VATICAN COUNCIL II

CONSTITUTION ON THE

CHURCH

VATICAN COUNCIL II

CONSTITUTION ON THE CHURCH

DE ECCLESIA
Proclaimed
November 21, 1964

FIDES PUBLISHERS, INC.
NOTRE DAME, INDIANA

NATIONAL CATHOLIC LAYMEN'S RETREAT CONFERENCE EDITION

This edition of the Constitution on the Church was prepared by Claude Leetham, IC, Council expert, and Campion Clifford, CP, moderator of the National Catholic Laymen's Retreat Conference.

Manufactured in the United States of America

PREFATORY NOTE

The immediate translations of the historic *Constitution on the Church* adopted in the third session of Vatican Council II were perhaps necessarily hasty. Much as the rushed translations of the liturgy diminished somewhat the first enthusiasm over the liturgical renewal, so inaccuracies and infelicities in the translation of the Council's important theological document impaired its impact and obscured momentarily its doctrinal and spiritual richness.

This was especially disappointing to the Catholic Laymen's Retreat Conference. Their national officers had voted to make the new Constitution the recommended source of points for meditation and for spiritual reading in affiliated retreat houses throughout the country for the indefinite future. It was the mind of the officers that nothing would more effectively assimilate the dogmatic concepts of the Constitution into the living texture of the spiritual lives of our generation than its immediate diffusion in lay retreat houses and the mastery of its content by meditation on its text.

The Moderator of the NCLRC, Father Campion Clifford, therefore gratefully welcomed the cooperation of Father Claude Leetham, the English Rosminian and Council expert, in the preparation of this version of the *Constitution on the Church*. Their brief notes introducing each chapter, relate every part of the Constitution to the spiritual life of the layman and add to the value of the careful and clear translation by which Fathers Leetham and Campion seek generously to serve retreatants and the wider reading public to whom, please God, the doctrine of Vatican Council II will bring intellectual refreshment, spiritual renewal and a more passionate love of Christ in his Church.

✠John Wright
Bishop of Pittsburgh
Episcopal Advisor, NCLRC

FEAST OF OUR LADY'S ASSUMPTION, 1965

CONTENTS

7

PAUL, BISHOP, SERVANT OF THE SERVANTS OF GOD TOGETHER WITH THE FATHERS OF THE SACRED COUNCIL

FOR A PERMANENT RECORD OF THE MATTER

DOGMATIC CONSTITUTION ON THE CHURCH

1.　　Christ is the Light of nations. It is therefore the eager desire of the Sacred Synod, gathered together in the Holy Spirit, to proclaim the Gospel to every creature and thus bring to all men the light of Christ which shines brightly on the countenance of the Church. Since the Church is in Christ like a sacrament or as a sign and instrument both of very closely knit union with God and of the unity of the whole human race, it desires now to unfold more fully to the faithful of the Church and to the whole world its own nature and universal mission. This it intends to do following faithfully the teaching of previous councils. The present day conditions of the world add greater urgency to this work of the Church so that all men, joined more closely today by various social, technical and cultural ties, may also attain fuller unity in Christ.

Introductory Note

This first chapter explains that the Church is a mystery in God's plan for the salvation of mankind. This simply means that while we are acquainted with the notion of the Church as an organized institution with a hierarchy, established legislative powers, etc., it is much more than just that, it is actually God working among men in the world today.

The Church has its origin in the love of the Blessed Trinity, and is a chosen people made one in the very unity of the Father, Son and Holy Spirit. It is the sign and instrument of God's plan for the union of God with mankind.

The Father sent his Son to redeem the world and to establish his kingdom here. This kingdom of Christ is the Church. His work of redemption did not cease with his death, but is continued in the sacrifice of the Mass, and the union of all believers is signified and effected by the Holy Eucharist.

All men are called to share this union for it is God's instrument of salvation for all mankind. Each of us has access to our heavenly Father through Christ by the action of the Holy Spirit, who dwells in the Church and in the hearts of the faithful.

The establishment of the Church as the kingdom of Christ was clearly foretold in the Old Testament, and after his resurrection, was established by the coming of the Holy Spirit. This Church has a special mission to perform, to spread the kingdom of Christ throughout the world. The Church is also the beginning of the restoration on earth of the kingdom of God, which is to be completed at the end of time. Then all things will be fulfilled in Christ and God's plan for mankind will be accomplished.

St. Paul teaches us that the Church is the mystical body of Christ. This first chapter explains in what sense this is to be understood. Christ is the head, the Holy Spirit is its life, the sacraments are its nourishment, and charity is its motivating force.

The Church is enriched with many special gifts and favors among which is the apostolic hierarchy. The Holy Spirit has given the hierarchy authority over the Church. The mystical body and the visible hierarchical Church are not two separate entities, but are really one and the same, having both a divine and a human element. The Holy Spirit reigns over the one and indivisible Church.

This Church, established by Christ in the world as a society, exists in the Catholic Church, with its hierarchical structure under the pope. However, there are many other elements of sanctification and truth found outside this visible structure of the Catholic Church. These elements actually belong to the Church and tend towards Catholic unity under the successor of St. Peter, the Vicar of Christ.

The Church follows Christ in suffering and persecution, and in love for the poor and afflicted. It uses Christ's methods of preaching, healing, reconciling. The Church is in a state of pilgrimage here on earth, announcing Christ's passion and death until the end of time.

Chapter I

THE MYSTERY OF
THE CHURCH

2.   The eternal Father, by a free and hidden plan of his own wisdom and goodness, created the whole world. His plan was to raise men to a sharing of the divine life. When man had fallen in Adam, God the Father did not leave man to himself, but constantly offered helps to salvation, in view of Christ, the Redeemer "who is the image of the invisible God, the firstborn of every creature" (Col 1: 15). All the elect, before time began, the Father "foreknew and predestined to become conformed to the image of his Son, that he should be the firstborn among many brethren" (Rom 8: 29). He planned to assemble in the holy Church all those who would believe in Christ. From the very beginning of the world the foreshadowing of the Church took place. It was prepared in a remarkable way throughout the history of the people of Israel and by means of the Old Covenant. In the present era of time the Church was constituted and, by the outpouring of the Spirit, was made manifest. At the end of time it will achieve glorious completion, when, as is read in the Fathers, all the just from Adam and "from Abel, the just one, to the last of the elect," will be gathered together with the Father in the universal Church.

The Kingdom of God Inaugurated

3.   The Son, therefore, came, sent by the Father. It was in him, before the foundation of the world, that the Father chose us and

predestined us to become adopted sons, for in him it pleased the Father to re-establish all things. (See Eph 1:4–5; 10). To carry out the will of the Father, Christ inaugurated the kingdom of heaven on earth and revealed to us the mystery of that kingdom. By his obedience he brought about redemption. The Church, or, in other words, the kingdom of Christ now present in mystery, grows visibly through the power of God in the world. This inauguration and this growth are symbolized by the blood and water which flowed from the open side of the crucified Jesus, and are foretold in the words of the Lord referring to his death on the cross: "And I, if I be lifted up from the earth will draw all things to myself" (John 12:32). As often as the sacrifice of the cross in which Christ our Passover was sacrificed is celebrated on the altar, the work of our redemption is carried on, and in the sacrament of the eucharistic bread, the unity of all believers who form one body in Christ is both expressed and brought about. All men are called to this union with Christ, who is the light of the world, from whom we come, through whom we live, and toward whom we direct our lives.

The Church Has Its Origin in the Blessed Trinity

4.   When the work which the Father gave the Son to do on earth was accomplished, the Holy Spirit was sent on the day of Pentecost in order that he might continually sanctify the Church, so that all who believe should have access through Christ in one Spirit to the Father. He is the Spirit of life, a fountain of water springing up to life eternal. To men, dead in sin, the Father gives life through him, until, in Christ, he brings to life their mortal bodies. The Spirit dwells in the Church and in the hearts of the faithful, as in a temple. In them he prays on their behalf and bears witness to the fact that they are adopted sons. The Spirit guides the Church in the way of all truth, unifies it in communion and works of ministry, and equips and directs it with hierarchical and charismatic gifts and adorns it with his fruits. By the power of the Gospel he makes the Church keep the freshness of youth. Uninterruptedly he renews it and leads it to perfect union with its spouse. The Spirit and the bride both say to Jesus, the Lord, "Come!"

Thus, the Church is seen as "a people made one with the unity of the father, the Son and the Holy Spirit" (St. Cyprian, *De Orat. Dom.*).

Beginning of the Kingdom

5.   The mystery of holy Church is manifest in its very foundation.

The Lord Jesus set it on its course by preaching the Good News, that is, the coming of the kingdom of God, which, for centuries, had been promised in the scriptures: "The time is fulfilled, and the kingdom of God is at hand" (Mark 1:15; See Matt 4:17). In the word, in the works, and in the presence of Christ, this kingdom was clearly open to the view of men. The Word of the Lord is compared to a seed which is sown in a field; those who hear the Word with faith and become part of the little flock of Christ have received the kingdom itself. Then, by its own power the seed sprouts and grows until harvest time. The miracles of Jesus also confirm that the kingdom has already arrived on earth: "If I cast out devils by the finger of God, then the kingdom of God has come upon you" (Luke 11:20; See Matt 12:28). Above all, however, the kingdom is clearly visible in the very person of Christ, the Son of God and the Son of Man, who came "to serve and to give his life as a ransom for many" (Mark 10:45).

The Kingdom Is To Be Spread by the Church

When Jesus, who had suffered the death of the cross for mankind, had risen, he appeared as the one constituted as Lord, Christ and eternal priest, and he poured out on his disciples the Spirit promised by the Father. From this source the Church, equipped with the gifts of its founder and faithfully guarding his precepts of charity, humility and self-sacrifice, receives the mission to proclaim and to spread among all peoples the kingdom of Christ and of God and to be, on earth, the initial budding forth of that kingdom. While it slowly grows, the Church strains toward the completed kingdom and, with all its strength, hopes and desires to be united in glory with its king.

Descriptive Symbols of the Kingdom

6.   Even as in the Old Testament the revelation of the kingdom is frequently conveyed in symbolic figure, so now the inner nature of the Church is made known to us by various images, taken from pastoral life, agriculture, building, or from family life, and marriage, which are suggested to us in the Books of the Prophets.

The Church is a *sheepfold* whose one and indispensable door is Christ. It is a flock of which God himself foretold he would be the shepherd, and whose sheep, although ruled by human shepherds, are nevertheless continuously led and nourished by Christ himself, the good shepherd and the prince of the shepherds, who gave his life for the sheep.

The Church is a piece of land to be cultivated, the *tillage* of God.

On that land the ancient olive tree grows whose holy roots were the prophets and in which the reconcilation of Jews and Gentiles is brought about and will be brought about. That land, like a choice vineyard, has been planted by the heavenly husbandman. The true vine is Christ who gives life and the power to bear abundant fruit to the branches, that is, to us, who through the Christ remain in Christ without whom we can do nothing.

Often the Church has also been called the *building* of God. The Lord himself compared himself to the stone which the builders rejected, but which was made into the cornerstone. On this foundation the Church is built by the apostles, and from it the Church receives durability and cohesion. This edifice has many names to describe it; the house of God in which dwells his family; the household of God in the Spirit; the dwelling place of God among men; and, especially, the holy *temple*. This temple, symbolized in places of worship built of stone, is praised by the holy Fathers and, not without reason, is compared in the liturgy to the holy city, the New Jerusalem. Here on earth we are built into it as living stones. John contemplates this holy city coming down from heaven at the renewal of the world as a bride made ready and adorned for her husband.

Or again, the Church, "that Jerusalem which is above," is also called "our mother." It is described as the spotless *spouse* of the spotless lamb, whom Christ "loved and for whom he delivered himself up that he might sanctify her" (Eph 5:26). He has united her to himself by an unbreakable covenant. He unceasingly "nourishes and cherishes" her. He cleansed her and joined her to himself, subject to him in love and fidelity. Finally, he filled her with heavenly gifts for all eternity, in order that we might know the love of God and of Christ for us, a love which surpasses all knowledge. The Church, while it journeys on earth in a foreign land away from the Lord, is like an exile. It seeks and experiences those things which are above, where Christ is seated at the right-hand of God, where the life of the Church is hidden with Christ in God until it appears in glory with its spouse.

The Mystical Body

7.   In the human nature united to himself the Son of God, by overcoming death through his own death and resurrection, redeemed man and re-fashioned him into a new creation. By communicating his spirit mystically, Christ made his brothers, called together from all nations, the components of his own body.

Christ's Life Permeates the Mystical Body

In this body the life of Christ is poured into the believers who, through the sacraments, are united in a hidden and real way to Christ who suffered and was glorified. Through baptism we are formed in the likeness of Christ: "For in one spirit we were all baptized into one body" (1 Cor 12:13). In this sacred rite a union with Christ's death and resurrection is both symbolized and brought about: "For we were buried with him by means of baptism into death," and if "we have been united with him in the likeness of his death, we shall be so in the likeness of his resurrection also" (Rom 6:4–5). Partaking really and truly of the body of the Lord in the breaking of the eucharistic bread, we are raised into fellowship with him and with one another. "Because the bread is one, we though many, are one body, all of us who partake of the one bread" (1 Cor 10:17). In this way all of us are made members of his body, but severally members of one another" (Rom 12:5).

Variety of Functions in the Mystical Body

As all the members of the human body, though they are many, form one body, so also are the faithful in Christ. Also, in the building up of Christ's body various members and functions have their part to play. There is only one Spirit who, according to his own richness and the needs of the ministries gives his different gifts for the welfare of the Church. Foremost among these gifts is the grace of the apostles to whose authority the Spirit himself has subjected even those who are endowed with charisms. This same Spirit produces and urges love among the believers giving the body unity by his own power and the close relationship of the members. From all this it follows that if one member endures anything, all the members endure it also, and if one member is honored, all the members rejoice together.

Christ the Head

The head of this body is Christ. He is the image of the invisible God and in him all things came into being. He is before all creatures and in him all things hold together. He is the head of the body which is the Church. He is the beginning, the first born from the dead, that in all things he might have the first place. By his immense power he rules the things in heaven and the things on earth, and with his all-surpassing perfection and action he fills the whole body with the riches of his glory.

Members Must Become Like Christ

All the members ought to be molded in the likeness of him, until Christ be formed in them. For this reason we, who have been made to conform with him, and have died with him and risen with him, are taken up into the mysteries of his life, until we will reign together with him. On earth, still as pilgrims in a strange land, tracing in trial and in oppression the paths he trod, we are made one with his sufferings as the body is one with the head, suffering with him, that with him we may be glorified.

Christ Enriches the Mystical Body

From him "the whole body, supplied and built up by joints and ligaments, attains a growth that is of God." He continually distributes in his body, that is, in the Church, gifts of ministries in which, by his own power, we serve each other unto salvation so that, carrying out the truth in love, we may through all things grow unto him who is our head.

The Work of the Holy Spirit

In order that we may be unceasingly renewed in him, he has shared with us his Spirit who, existing as one and the same being in the head and in the members, vivifies, unifies and moves through the whole body. This he does in such a way that his work could be compared by the holy Fathers with the function which the principle of life, that is, the soul, fulfills in the human body.

The Church the Bride of Christ

Christ loves the Church as his bride, having become the model of a man loving his wife as his body; the Church, indeed, is subject to its head. "Because in him dwells all the fullness of the Godhead bodily" (Col 2:9), he fills the Church, which is his body and his fullness, with his divine gifts so that it may expand and reach all the fullness of God.

The Church Visible and Invisible Is One

8.   Christ, the one mediator, established here on earth his holy Church which he unfailingly sustains as a community of faith, hope and charity, a visible organization through which he communicates truth and grace to all. But, the society which is endowed with hierarchical organs and the mystical body of Christ are not to be considered as two realities. The same is true of the impressive assembly of

the faithful and the spiritual community, and of the earthly Church and the Church enriched with heavenly gifts. These form one complex reality which consists of a divine and a human element. For this reason, by a valid analogy, it is compared to the mystery of the incarnate Word. As the assumed nature inseparably united to him serves the divine Word as a living organ of salvation, so, in a similar way, does the visible social structure of the Church serve the Spirit of Christ, who vivifies it, in the building up of the body.

The One Church of Christ

This is the one Church of Christ which in the Creed is professed as one, holy, catholic and apostolic, which our Savior, after his resurrection, commissioned Peter to shepherd, and with the other apostles to extend and rule, establishing it for all ages as "the pillar and mainstay of truth" (1 Tim 3:15). This Church, constituted and organized in the world as a society, exists in the Catholic Church, which is governed by the successor of Peter and by the bishops in communion with him, although many elements of sanctification and of truth are found outside of its visible structure. These elements, as gifts belonging to the Church of Christ, are forces impelling toward catholic unity.

The Church Employs Christ's Methods

Just as Christ carried out the work of redemption in poverty and persecution, so the Church is called to follow the same path that it may communicate the fruits of salvation to men. Christ Jesus, "though he was by nature God . . . emptied himself, taking the nature of a slave" (Phil 2:6), and "being rich, became poor" (2 Cor 8:9) for our sakes. Thus, the Church, although it needs human resources to carry out its mission, is not set up to seek earthly glory, but to proclaim, by its own example, humility and self-sacrifice. Christ was sent by the Father "to bring good news to the poor, to heal the contrite of heart" (Luke 4:18) "to seek and to save what was lost" (Luke 19:10). Similarly, the Church encompasses with love all who are afflicted with human suffering and in the poor and afflicted sees the image of its poor and suffering founder. It does all it can to relieve their need and in them it strives to serve Christ. As Christ, holy, innocent and undefiled knew nothing of sin, but only came to expiate the sins of the people, so the Church, cherishing sinners in her midst is holy yet always in need of being purified and continually follows the way of penance and renewal. The Church, "like a stranger in a foreign land, presses forward amid the persecutions of the world and the consolations of God" (St. Augustine, *Civ.Dei.*), announcing the cross and death of the Lord until he comes. By the power of the risen Lord it is given strength that it may, in patience and in love, overcome its sorrows and its challenges, both within and from without, and may reveal to the world, faithfully though darkly, the mystery of its Lord until finally it is manifested in full light.

Introductory Note   Chapter II

In the first chapter we saw that the Church has its beginning in the love of the Blessed Trinity, and is a chosen people. It is known as the people of God. This second chapter expands this idea and explains the nature and function of the people of God.

The theme of this chapter is that union of love between the people of God and God himself begun in the Old Testament and ennobled and enriched by the new and perfect convenant of the New Testament in the blood of Christ. It describes God's dealing with mankind in history. Christ is the head of this chosen people, for he established the kingdom of God on earth, and through and with his people, will bring it to perfection. This new people of God, then, is the Church, uniting all in a fellowship of life, charity and truth.

Membership of this kingdom comes through baptism and is completed in confirmation. All members share in the priestly, prophetic and kingly office of Christ. The priesthood of the ordained clergy, however, differs in essence from that of the laity by reason of the special sacrament of Holy Orders that the latter receive. Yet the common priesthood of the laity and the ministerial priesthood of the clergy are definitely interrelated, each being in its own special way a sharing in the priesthood of Christ.

Through the sacraments the people of God are able to live the very life of the Holy Trinity. This people which is organized for its mission has a variety of endowments and gifts and each member has a contribution to make to God's plan. And this is the holiness to which every member is called.

All men are called to be a part of the people of God and to find their salvation through the Church. Although all religions are linked to the Church by their love of God or of Christ, the Church still must seek to make known all the truths confided to it.

Chapter II

THE PEOPLE OF GOD

9.   At all times and in every race God has given welcome to who-soever fears him and does what is right. God, however, does not make men holy and save them merely as individuals, without bond or link between one another. Rather has it pleased him to bring men together as one people, a people which acknowledges him in truth and serves him in holiness. He therefore chose the Israelites as a people unto himself. With it he set up a covenant. Step by step he taught and prepared this people, making known in its history both himself and the decree of his will and making it holy unto himself. All these things, however, were done by way of preparation and as a figure of that new and perfect covenant, which was to be rati-fied in Christ, and of that fuller revelation which was to be given through the Word of God himself made flesh. "Behold the days shall come saith the Lord, and I will make a new covenant with the House of Israel, and with the house of Judah . . . I will give my law in their bowels, and I will write it in their heart, and I will be their God, and they shall be my people . . . For all of them shall know me, from the least of them even to the greatest, saith the Lord" (Jer 31:31–34). Christ instituted this new covenant, the new testament, in his blood, calling together a people made up of Jew and Gentile, making them one, not according to the flesh but in the Spirit. This was to be the new people of God. For those who believe in Christ, who are reborn not from a perishable but from an imperishable seed through the word of the living God (See 1 Pet 1:23) not from the

flesh but from water and the Holy Spirit, are finally established as "a chosen race, a royal priesthood, a holy nation, a purchased people . . . who in times past were not a people, but are now the people of God" (1 Pet 2:9–10).

The People of God the Instrument of Salvation

That messianic people has Christ for its head, "who was delivered up for our sins, and rose again for our justification" (Rom 4:25), and now having won a name which is above all names, reigns in glory in heaven. This people has the dignity and freedom of the sons of God, in whose hearts the Holy Spirit dwells as in his temple. Its law is the new commandment to love as Christ loved us. Its end is the kingdom of God, which has been begun by God himself on earth, and which is to be further extended until it is brought to perfection by him at the end of time, when Christ, our life, shall appear, and "creation itself will be delivered from its slavery to corruption into the freedom of the glory of the sons of God" (Rom 8:21). Thus the messianic people, although it does not actually include all men, and at times may look like a small flock, is nonetheless a lasting and sure seed of unity, hope and salvation for the whole human race. Established by Christ as a communion of life, charity and truth, it is also used by him as an instrument for the redemption of all, and is sent forth into the whole world as the light of the world and the salt of the earth.

The People of God in the Church of Christ

Israel according to the flesh, which wandered as an exile in the desert, was already called the Church of God. So likewise the new Israel which while living in this present age goes in search of a future and abiding city, is called the Church of Christ. For he has bought it for himself with his blood, has filled it with his Spirit and provided it with those means which befit it as a visible and social union. God gathered together as one all those who in faith look upon Jesus as the author of salvation and the source of unity and peace. He established them as the Church, that for each and for all it may be the visible sacrament of this saving unity. While it transcends all limits of time and confines of race, the Church is destined to extend to all regions of the earth and so enters into the history of mankind. Moving forward through trial and tribulation, the Church is strengthened by the power of God's grace, which was promised to her by the Lord, so that in the weakness of the flesh she may not waver from perfect fidelity, but remain a bride worthy of her Lord, and moved by the Holy Spirit may never cease to renew herself, until through the cross she arrives at the light which knows no setting.

Baptism and Confirmation Establish a Priestly People

10.   Christ the Lord, the high priest taken from among men made the new people "a kingdom and priests to God the Father" (See Apoc 1:6; 5:9–10). The baptized, by regeneration and the anointing of the Holy Spirit, are consecrated as a spiritual house and a holy priesthood, in order that through every activity of the Christian they may offer spiritual sacrifices and proclaim the power of him who has called them out of darkness into his marvelous light. Therefore all the disciples of Christ, persevering in prayer and praising God, should present themselves as a living sacrifice, holy and pleasing to God. Everywhere on earth they must bear witness to Christ and give an answer to those who request an account of that hope of eternal life which is in them.

The Priesthood of the Ordained and of the Faithful Are Interrelated

Though they differ from one another in essence and not only in degree, the common priesthood of the faithful and the ministerial or hierarchical priesthood are nonetheless interrelated: each of them in its own special way is a participation in the one priesthood of Christ. The ministerial priest, by the sacred power he enjoys, teaches and rules the priestly people; acting in the person of Christ, he makes present the eucharistic sacrifice, and offers it to God in the name of all the people. The faithful, on the other hand, in virtue of their royal priesthood, join in the offering of the Eucharist. They likewise exercise that priesthood in receiving the sacraments, in prayer and thanksgiving, in the witness of a holy life, and by self-denial and active charity.

The Sacraments Activate the Priestly Office

11.   It is through the sacraments and the exercise of the virtues that the sacred nature and organic structure of the priestly community is brought into operation. Incorporated in the Church through baptism, the faithful are destined by the baptismal character for the worship of the Christian religion; reborn as sons of God they must confess before men the faith which they have received from God through the Church. They are even more perfectly bound to the Church by the sacrament of confirmation, and the Holy Spirit endows them with special strength, and this obliges them more strictly to spread and defend the faith, both by word and by deed,

as true witnesses of Christ. Taking part in the eucharistic sacrifice, which is the fount and apex of the whole Christian life, they offer the divine victim to God, and offer themselves along with it. Thus both by reason of the offering and through holy Communion all take part in this liturgical service, not indeed, all in the same way but each in the way which is proper to himself. Strengthened in holy Communion by the body of Christ, they then manifest in a concrete way that unity of the people of God which is suitably signified and wondrously brought about by this most august sacrament.

Penance, Anointing, Orders

Those who approach the sacrament of penance obtain pardon from the mercy of God for the offense committed against him and are at the same time reconciled with the Church, which they have wounded by their sins, and which by charity, example, and prayer seeks their conversion. By the sacred anointing of the sick and the prayer of her priests the whole Church commends the sick to the suffering and glorified Lord, asking that he may lighten their suffering and save them; she exhorts them, moreover, to contribute to the welfare of the whole people of God by associating themselves freely with the passion and death of Christ. Those of the faithful who are consecrated by holy orders are appointed to feed the Church in Christ's name with the word and the grace of God.

Matrimony Perpetuates the People of God

Finally, Christian spouses, in virtue of the sacrament of matrimony, whereby they signify and share in the mystery of that unity and fruitful love which exists between Christ and his Church, help each other to attain to holiness in their married life and in the rearing and education of their children. By reason of their state and way of life they have their own special gift among the people of God. From the wedlock of Christians there comes the family, in which new citizens of human society are born, who by the grace of the Holy Spirit, received in baptism, are made children of God, thus perpetuating the people of God through the centuries. The family is, so to speak, the domestic Church. In it parents should, by their word and example, be the first preachers of the faith to their children; they should encourage them in the vocation which is proper to each of them, fostering with special care a vocation to a sacred state.

All Are Called to Perfect Holiness

Fortified by so many and such powerful means of salvation, all the faithful, whatever their condition or state, are called by the Lord, each in his own way, to that perfect holiness whereby the Father himself is perfect.

The People of God Witness to Christ

12.   The holy people of God shares also in Christ's prophetic office; it spreads abroad a living witness to him, especially by means of a life of faith and charity and by offering to God a sacrifice of praise, the tribute of lips which give praise to his name. The entire body of the faithful, anointed as they are by the holy one, cannot err in matters of belief. They manifest this special property by means of the whole people's supernatural discernment in matters of faith when, "from the bishops down to the last of the lay faithful" (St. Augustine, *De Praed. Sanct.*) they show universal agreement in matters of faith and morals. This discernment in matters of faith is aroused and sustained by the Spirit of truth. It is exercised under the guidance of the sacred teaching authority, in faithful and respectful obedience to which the people of God accepts what is not just the word of men but the true word of God. By this means the people of God adheres unwaveringly to the faith given once and for all to the saints, with unfailing judgment penetrates more deeply into its mystery and applies it more fully to its life.

Variety of Gifts

It is not only through the sacraments and the ministries of the Church that the Holy Spirit sanctifies and leads the people of God and enriches it with virtues, but, "allotting his gifts to everyone according as he wills" (1 Cor 12:11), he distributes special graces among the faithful of every rank. By these gifts he makes them fit and ready to undertake the various tasks and offices which contribute toward the renewal and building up of the Church, according to the words of the Apostle: "The manifestation of the Spirit is given to everyone for profit (1 Cor 12:7). These charisms, whether they be outstanding or more simple and commonplace, are to be received with thanksgiving and consolation, for they are precisely suited to the needs of the Church and useful for its work. Extraordinary gifts are not to be sought after, nor are the results of apostolic labor to be presumptuously expected from their possession but judgment as to their genuineness and proper use belongs to those who are appointed leaders in the Church, to whose special competence it belongs, not indeed to extinguish the Spirit, but to test all things and hold fast to that which is good.

The Holy Trinity Unites the People of God

13.   All men are called to belong to the new people of God. Wherefore this people, while remaining one and only one, is to be spread throughout the whole world and must exist in all ages, so that the decree of God's will may be fulfilled. In the beginning God made human nature one and decreed that all his children, scattered as they were should finally be gathered together as one. It was for this purpose that God sent his Son, whom he appointed heir of all things, that he might be teacher, king and priest of all, the head of the new and universal people of the sons of God. For this too God sent the Spirit of his Son as Lord and life-giver. He it is who brings together the whole Church and each and every one of those who believe, and who is the principle of their unity in the teaching of the apostles and in fellowship, in the breaking of bread and in prayer.

The People of God Is Universal

It follows that though there are many nations there is but one people of God, which takes its citizens from every race, making them citizens of a kingdom which is of a heavenly rather than of an earthly nature. All the faithful, scattered though they be throughout the world, are in communion with each other in the Holy Spirit, and so "he who dwells in Rome knows that the people of India are his members" (St. John Chrysostom, *Hom. 65*). Since the kingdom of Christ is not of this world the Church or people of God in establishing that kingdom takes nothing away from the temporal welfare of any people. On the contrary, insofar as they are good, it fosters and makes use of the ability, resources and customs in which the genius of each people expresses itself. By so doing it purifies, strengthens, elevates and ennobles them. The Church in this is mindful that she must bring together the nations for that king to whom they were given as an inheritance, and to whose city they bring gifts and offerings. This characteristic of universality which adorns the people of God is a gift from the Lord himself. By reason of it, the Catholic Church strives constantly and effectively to bring all humanity and all its possessions back to its source in Christ, with him as its head in the unity of his Spirit.

The Church Has Unity in Diversity

In virtue of this catholicity each individual part contributes through its special gifts to the good of the other parts and of the whole Church. Through the common sharing of gifts and through the common effort to attain fullness in unity, the whole and each of the parts receive increase. The people of God, then, is not only made up of different peoples, but in its inner structure also it is composed of various orders. This diversity among its members arises either by reason of their duties, as is the case with those who exercise the sacred ministry for the good of their brethren, or by reason of their condition and state of life. This is the case of those many who enter the religious state, and, tending toward holiness by a narrow path, stimulate their brethren by their example. Moreover, within the Church particular Churches hold a rightful place; these Churches retain their own traditions, without in any way opposing the primacy of the Chair of Peter, which presides over the whole assembly of charity and protects sanctioned variety. At the same time it guarantees that such variety does not hinder unity but rather contributes towards it. Between all the parts of the Church there remains a bond of close communion whereby they share spiritual riches, apostolic workers and temporal resources. For the members of the people of God are called to share these goods in common, and of each of the Churches the words of the apostle hold good: "According to the gift that each has received, administer it to one another as good stewards of the manifold grace of God" (1 Pet 4:10).

All Mankind Is Related to the People of God

All men are called to be part of this catholic unity of the people of God which promotes universal peace and is its herald. The Catholic faithful, all who believe in Christ, and indeed the whole of mankind, belong to or are related to it in various ways, for all men are called by the grace of God to salvation.

The Church Is Necessary for Salvation

14.   This Sacred Council first considers the Catholic faithful. Basing itself upon Sacred Scripture and Tradition, it teaches that the Church, now sojourning on earth in exile, is necessary for salvation. Christ, present to us in his Body, which is the Church, is the one mediator and the only way of salvation. In explicit terms he himself affirmed the necessity of faith and baptism and thereby affirmed also the necessity of the Church, for through baptism as through a door men enter the Church. Whosoever, therefore, knowing that the Catholic Church was made necessary by Christ, refuses to enter it or remain in it, cannot be saved.

Full Membership of the Church

Those are fully incorporated in the society of the Church who, possessing the Spirit of Christ, accept its entire system and all the means of salvation which it possesses. They are united with it as part of its visible structure and through it with Christ, who rules it through the Supreme Pontiff and the bishops. The bonds that join men to the Church in a visible way are profession of faith, the sacraments, and ecclesiastical government and communion. He is not saved, however, who though part of the body of the Church, does not persevere in charity. He remains indeed in the bosom of the Church, but, as it were, only in a "bodily" manner and not "in his heart." All the Church's children should remember that their exalted status is to be attributed not to their own merits, but to the special grace of Christ. If they fail moreover to respond to that grace in thought, word and deed, not only will they not be saved, but they will be the more severely judged.

Catechumens

Catechumens who, moved by the Holy Spirit, seek with explicit intention to be incorporated into the Church, are by that very intention joined with her. With love and solicitude Mother Church already embraces them as her own.

All the Baptized Are Linked with the Church

15.   The Church recognizes that in many ways she is linked with those who, being baptized, are honored with the name of Christian, though they do not profess the faith in its entirety or do not preserve unity of communion with the successor of Peter. For there are many who honor Sacred Scripture, taking it as a norm of belief and a pattern of life, and who show a sincere zeal. They have a loving faith in God the Father Almighty and in Christ, the Son of God and Savior. They are consecrated by baptism by which they are united with Christ. They also recognize and accept other sacraments within their own Churches or ecclesiastical communities. Many of them possess the episcopate, celebrate the Holy Eucharist and cultivate devotion toward the Virgin Mother of God. They also share with us in prayer and other spiritual benefits. Moreover we may say that in some real way they are joined with us in the Holy Spirit, for to them also he gives his gifts and graces for he works in them with his sanctifying power. Some indeed he has strengthened to the extent of the shedding of their blood. In all Christ's disciples the Spirit is arousing a desire accompanied by action for peaceful union in the manner determined by Christ, as one flock under one shepherd. Mother Church never ceases to pray, hope and work that this may come

about. She exhorts her children to purification and renewal so that the sign of Christ may shine more brightly over the face of the earth.

Non-Christians

16.   Finally, those who have not yet received the Gospel are related in various ways to the people of God. In the first place we must recall the people to whom the testament and the promises were given and from whom Christ was born according to the flesh. For the sake of their fathers this people remains most dear to God, for God does not repent of the gifts he makes nor of the calls he issues. The plan of salvation also includes those who acknowledge the Creator. In the first place among these there are the Mohammedans, who, professing to hold the faith of Abraham adore with us the one and merciful God, who on the last day will judge mankind. Nor is God far distant from those who in shadows and images seek the unknown God, for it is he who gives to all men life and breath and all things, and as Savior, wills that all men be saved. Those also can attain to salvation who through no fault of their own do not know the Gospel of Christ or his Church, yet sincerely seek God and, moved by grace, strive by their deeds to do his will as it is known to them through the dictates of conscience. Nor does divine Providence deny the helps necessary for salvation to those who, without blame on their part, have not yet arrived at an explicit knowledge of God and with his grace strive to live a good life. Whatever good or truth is found among them is looked upon by the Church as a preparation for the Gospel. She knows that it is given by him who enlightens all men so that they may finally have life. Too often men, deceived by the Evil One, have become vain in their reasonings and have exchanged the truth of God for a lie, serving the creature rather than the Creator. Some there are who, living and dying in this world without God, are exposed to final despair. For this reason, mindful of the command of the Lord, "Preach the Gospel to every creature" (Mark 16:16), the Church diligently fosters the missions for the glory of God and for the salvation of all these souls.

The Church Must Be Missionary

17.   As the Son was sent by the Father, so he too sent the apostles, saying: "Go therefore, make disciples of all nations, baptizing them in the name of the Father and of the Son and of the Holy Spirit, teaching them to observe all things whatsoever I have commanded you. And behold I am with you all days even to the consummation of the world" (Matt 21:18–20). This solemn mandate of

Christ to proclaim the saving truth has been handed on by the apostles and the Church must carry it out to the very ends of the earth. Wherefore it makes the words of the Apostle its own: "Woe to me, if I do not preach the Gospel" (1 Cor 9:16), and continues unceasingly to send heralds of the Gospel until such time as the infant churches are fully established and can themselves continue the work of evangelizing. For the Church is compelled by the Holy Spirit to do its part that God's plan may be fully realized, whereby he has constituted Christ as the source of salvation for the whole world. By the proclamation of the Gospel it prepares its hearers to receive and profess the faith. It gives them the dispositions necessary for baptism, snatches them from the slavery of error and of idols, and incorporates them in Christ so that through charity they may grow up into full maturity in Christ. Through its work, whatever good is in the minds and hearts of men, whatever good lies latent in the religious practices and cultures of diverse peoples, is not only saved from destruction but is also cleansed, raised up and perfected unto the glory of God, the confusion of the devil and the happiness of man. The obligation of spreading the faith is imposed on every disciple of Christ, according to his state. Anyone can baptize those who believe, but the priest alone can complete the building of the body in the eucharistic sacrifice. Thus are fulfilled the words of God, spoken through his prophet: "From the rising of the sun until the going down thereof my name is great among the Gentiles, and in every place a clean oblation is sacrificed and offered up in my name" (Mal 1:11). In this way the Church both prays and labors in order that the entire world may become the people of God, the body of the Lord and the temple of the Holy Spirit, and that in Christ, the head of all, all honor and glory may be rendered to the Creator and Father of all mankind.

Introductory Note   Chapter III

The first Vatican Council was suspended in 1870 because of the outbreak of the Franco-Prussian war. Thus the work of the Council was not completed. It had clearly defined the primacy of the pope as the successor of St. Peter and visible head of the Church, with infallible judgment in matters of faith and morals. However, the Council did not have time to make clear and definite the role and function of the bishops, successors of the other apostles. This present Council has now completed the work. Chapter III declares in clear terms the place of bishops in Christ's Church. It shows how the bishops are the principle of unity in the Church, making Christ present to the faithful by their teaching, governing and sanctifying.

Together with the pope, the bishops form a college that rules the Church of God. They derive the fulness of their priestly power from their consecration, and their jurisdiction (at least in the West) from the pope. There are many groups of local churches in the universal Church, yet the unity that exists among them all is their individual and collective unity with the pope.

This chapter stresses the presence of Christ and of the whole Church in every diocese and local community. This presence is made possible through the priesthood, that is through the bishop and through the priests and other ministers who are his helpers.

Infallibility is the personal prerogative of the pope, but the College of Bishops in communion with the pope also share it, hence it is shown that the Church itself has this special attribute of infallibility which keeps it free from error.

After a detailed description of the role and function of bishops and their relations with their flocks, this chapter then treats of priests and deacons and their duties and functions.

The constant underlying theme of Chapter III is unity—a unity of pope and bishops, of bishops with one another, of bishops and priests, of clergy and laity.

Chapter III

ON THE HIERARCHICAL STRUCTURE OF THE CHURCH AND IN PARTICULAR ON THE EPISCOPATE

18.   For the nurturing and constant growth of the people of God, Christ the Lord instituted in his Church a variety of ministries, which work for the good of the whole body. Indeed those ministers, who are endowed with sacred power, serve their brethren, so that all the members of the people of God, who thereby enjoy its true Christian dignity, may work towards the common goal of salvation, freely and in an orderly way.

The Council Reaffirms the Teaching of Vatican I

This Sacred Council, following closely in the footsteps of the First Vatican Council, teaches and declares that Jesus Christ, the eternal shepherd, established his holy Church, having sent forth the apostles as he himself had been sent by the Father, and he willed that their successors, namely the bishops, should be shepherds in his Church even to the consummation of the world. And in order that the episcopate itself might be one and undivided, he placed blessed Peter over the other apostles, and instituted in him a permanent and visible source and foundation of unity of faith and communion. And all this teaching about the institution, the perpetuity, the meaning and the reason for the sacred primacy of the Roman Pontiff and of his infallible magisterium, this Sacred Council again proposes to be firmly believed by all the faithful. Proceeding a step further, this Council has decided to declare and proclaim before all men the doctrine concerning bishops, the successors of the apostles, who together with the successor of Peter, the Vicar of Christ, the visible Head of the whole Church, govern the house of the living God.

The Apostolic College

19.   The Lord Jesus, after praying to the Father, called to himself those whom he desired, and appointed twelve to be with him, whom he would send to preach the kingdom of God. He established these apostles after the manner of a college or a stable group, over which he placed Peter chosen from among them. He sent them first to the children of Israel and then to all nations, so that as sharers in his power they might make all peoples his disciples, and sanctify and govern them. Thus they would spread his Church, and by ministering to it under the guidance of the Lord, direct it all days even to the consummation of the world. In this mission they were fully confirmed on the day of Pentecost in accordance with the Lord's promise: "You shall receive power when the Holy Spirit comes upon you, and you shall be witnesses for me in Jerusalem, and in Judea and in Samaria, and even to the very ends of the earth" (Acts 1:8). By preaching the Gospel everywhere, and by its acceptance by their hearers under the influence of the Holy Spirit, the apostles gather together the universal Church, which the Lord founded on the apostles and built upon blessed Peter, their chief, Christ Jesus himself being the supreme cornerstone.

The Divine Mission Will Last until the End of the World

20.   That divine mission, entrusted by Christ to the apostles, will last until the end of the world, since the Gospel they are to teach is for all time the source of all life for the Church. For this reason the apostles in this hierarchically established society took care to appoint successors.

The Apostles Appointed Successors

The apostles not only had helpers in their ministry, but also, in order that the mission assigned to them might continue after their death, they passed on to their immediate cooperators, as if in the form of a testament, the duty of confirming and finishing the work begun by themselves, recommending to them that they attend to the whole flock in which the Holy Spirit placed them to shepherd the Church of God. They therefore appointed such men, and ordered that after their death other approved men should take up their ministry. Among the various ministries according to tradition in the Church from the earliest times, the chief place belongs to the office of those who are appointed to the episcopate. By a succession which has its origin from the very beginning, they derive their apostolic life from their predecessors who have transmitted it to them. Thus, as St. Irenaeus testifies, through those who were appointed bishops by the apostles, and through their successors down to our own time, the apostolic tradition is manifested and preserved.

Bishops, Successors to the Apostles

Bishops, therefore, with their helpers, the priests and deacons, have undertaken the service of the community, presiding in place of God over the flock, whose shepherds they are, as teachers for doctrine, priests for sacred worship, and ministers for governing. Just as the office granted individually to Peter, the first among the apostles, is permanent and is to be transmitted to his successors, so also the apostles' office of nurturing the Church is permanent, and is to be exercised without interruption by the sacred order of bishops. Therefore, the Sacred Council teaches that bishops by divine institution have succeeded to the place of the apostles, as shepherds of the Church, and he who hears them, hears Christ, and he who rejects them, rejects Christ and him who sent Christ.

The Bishops Attest to the Presence of Christ

21.   In the bishops, therefore, to whom priests are assistants, our Lord Jesus Christ, the supreme high priest, is present in the midst of those who believe. Though he sits at the right hand of God the Father, he is not absent for the gathering of his high priests, but chiefly through their exalted service he is preaching the word of God to all nations, and constantly administering the sacraments of faith to those who believe. Through their paternal functions he incorporates new members into his body by a heavenly regeneration, and finally by their wisdom and prudence he directs and guides the people of the New Testament in their pilgrimage toward eternal happiness. These pastors, chosen to shepherd the Lord's flock of the elect, are servants of Christ and stewards of the mysteries of God, and to them has been assigned the duty of witnessing to the Gospel

of the grace of God, and the ministration of the Spirit and of justice in glory.

The Episcopate, the Plentitude of Orders

For the discharge of such great duties, the apostles were enriched by Christ with a special outpouring of the Holy Spirit coming upon them, and it has been transmitted down to us by episcopal consecration. The Sacred Council teaches that by episcopal consecration the fullness of the sacrament of orders is conferred, namely, that fullness of power, which both in the church's liturgical practice and in the language of the Fathers of the Church is called the high priesthood, the supreme power of the sacred ministry. But episcopal consecration confers together with the office of sanctification, the functions of teaching and of ruling, though, by their nature, they cannot be exercised except in hierarchical communion with the head and members of the college. From the tradition, which is expressed especially in liturgical rites and in the practice of both the Church of the East and of the West, it is clear that, by means of the imposition of hands and the words of consecration, the grace of the Holy Spirit is conferred, and the sacred character impressed, in such a way that bishops in an eminent and visible way sustain the role of Christ himself as teacher, shepherd and high priest, and that they act in his person. It pertains to the bishops to admit newly elected members into the episcopal body by means of the sacrament of orders.

Collegiality in History

22.   By our Lord's ordinance, St. Peter and the other apostles are constituted one apostolic college. In like manner the Roman Pontiff, the successor of Peter, and the bishops, the successors of the apostles, are bound in union. Indeed, the collegiate character and functioning of the episcopal order is indicated by the very ancient practice whereby bishops, established in every part of the world, were in communion with one another and with the bishop of Rome, in a bond of unity, charity and peace. The same thing can be seen in assembled councils, where profound issues were settled in common after carefully considering the opinions expressed by many bishops. Ecumenical Councils held in the course of centuries are another evident proof of the collegiate character of the episcopate. It is intimated also in the practice, introduced in ancient times, of summoning several bishops to take part in the elevation of the newly elected to the ministry of the high priesthood. Hence, a man is constituted a member of the episcopal body in virtue of sacramen-

tal consecration and hierarchical communion with the head and members of the body.

The Pope and the Episcopal College

But the college or body of bishops has no authority unless the term is understood to mean that their authority is exercised together with the Roman Pontiff, the successor of Peter, and that his power of primacy over all, bishops and faithful, is maintained in its entirety. In virtue of his office, that is as Vicar of Christ and pastor of the whole Church, the Roman Pontiff has full, supreme and universal power over the Church, and he is always free to exercise this power. The order of bishops, which succeeds to the college of apostles and gives this apostolic body continued existence, is also the subject of supreme and full power over the universal Church, provided we understand this body together with its head the Roman Pontiff and never without this head. This power can be exercised only with the consent of the Roman Pontiff, for our Lord placed Simon alone as the rock and the bearer of the keys of the Church, and made him shepherd of the whole flock. It is evident, however, that the power of binding and loosing, which was given to Peter, was granted also to the college of apostles, joined with their head. This college, insofar as it is composed of many, expresses the variety and universality of the people of God, but insofar as it is assembled under one head, it expresses the unity of the flock of Christ. In this college, the bishops, faithfully recognizing the primacy and pre-eminence of their head, exercise their own authority for the good of their own faithful, and indeed of the whole Church, while the Holy Spirit unfailingly strengthens its organic structure and internal harmony. The supreme power in the universal Church, which this college enjoys, is exercised in a solemn way in an ecumenical council. A council is never ecumenical unless it is confirmed or at least accepted as such by the successor of Peter; and it is prerogative of the Roman Pontiff to convoke these councils, to preside over them and to confirm them. This same collegiate power can be exercised together with the pope by the bishops living in all parts of the world, provided that the head of the college calls them to collegiate action, or at least approves of or freely accepts the united action of the scattered bishops, so that it is thereby made a collegiate act.

Through the Bishops the Universal Church Is Localized

23.   This collegial union is apparent also in the mutual relations of the individual bishops with particular churches and with the uni-

versal Church. The Roman Pontiff as the successor of Peter, is the permanent and visible principle and foundation of unity of both bishops and faithful. The individual bishops, however, are the visible principle and foundation of unity in their particular churches. These churches are fashioned after the model of the universal Church. In them and from them comes the one and only Catholic Church. For this reason each individual bishop represents his own church, but all of them together and with the pope represent the entire Church in the bond of peace, love and unity.

Every Bishop Cares for the Whole Church

The individual bishops, who are placed in charge of particular churches, exercise their pastoral government over the portion of the people of God committed to their care, and not over other churches nor over the universal Church. But each of them, as a member of the episcopal college and legitimate successor of the apostles, is obliged by Christ's institution and command to be solicitous for the whole Church. This solicitude, though it is not exercised by an act of jurisdiction, contributes greatly to the advantage of the universal Church. For it is the duty of all bishops to promote and safeguard the unity of faith and the discipline common to the whole Church, to instruct the faithful to love the whole mystical body of Christ, especially its poor and sorrowing members and those who are suffering persecution for justice's sake.

Finally, they must promote every activity that is common to the whole Church, especially that the faith may increase and the light of full truth appear to all men. It is a contribution to holiness, that by governing well their own church as a portion of the universal Church, they are effectively contributing to the welfare of the whole mystical body, which is also the body of the Churches.

Cooperation Among Bishops

The task of proclaiming the Gospel everywhere on earth pertains to the body of bishops, to all of whom in common Christ gave his command, thereby imposing upon them a common duty, as Pope Celestine in his time recommended to the Fathers of the Council of Ephesus. From this it follows that the individual bishops, insofar as their own discharge of their duty permits, are obliged to enter into a community of work among themselves and with the successor of Peter, upon whom was imposed in a special way the great duty of spreading the Christian name. With all their energy, therefore, they must supply to the missions both workers for the harvest and also

spiritual and material aid, both directly as well as by arousing the
active cooperation of the faithful. Finally, the bishops, in a universal
fellowship of charity, should gladly extend their fraternal aid to
other churches, especially to neighboring and more needy dioceses
in accordance with the venerable example of antiquity.

Variety of Local Churches

By divine Providence it has come about that various churches,
established in various places by the apostles and their successors,
have in the course of time coalesced into several groups, organically
united, which, preserving the unity of faith and the one divine constitution of the universal Church, enjoy their own discipline, their
own liturgical usage, and their own theological and spiritual herit-
age. Some of these Churches, notably the ancient patriarchal
Churches, as parent-stocks, so to speak, of the faith, have begotten
others as daughter Churches, with which they are connected down
to our own time by a close bond of charity in their sacramental life
and in their mutual respect for their rights and duties. The agreement in diversity of local churches is splendid evidence of the catholicity of the undivided Church. In like manner the episcopal bodies
of today are in a position to render a manifold and fruitful service,
so that this collegiate awareness may have practical application.

The Mission of Bishops Is a Service

24.   Bishops, as successors of the apostles, receive from the Lord,
to whom was given all power in heaven and on earth, the mission to
teach all nations and to preach the Gospel to every creature, so that
all men may attain to salvation by faith, baptism and the fulfillment
of the commandments. To fulfill this mission Christ the Lord promised the Holy Spirit to the apostles, and on Pentecost sent the Spirit
from heaven, by whose power they would be witnesses to him before the nations and peoples and kings and even to the ends of the
earth. That duty, which the Lord committed to the shepherds of his
people, is a true service, which in sacred literature is significantly
called "diakonia" or ministry.

How Bishops Receive Jurisdiction

The canonical mission of bishops can come about by lawful customs that have not been revoked by the supreme and universal
authority of the Church, or by laws made or recognized by that same
authority, or directly through the successor of Peter himself; and

if the latter refuses or denies apostolic communion, such bishops cannot assume any office.

Teaching Office of Bishops

25.   Among the principal duties of bishops the preaching of the Gospel occupies an eminent place. For bishops are preachers of the faith, who lead new disciples to Christ, and are authentic teachers, that is, teachers endowed with the authority of Christ. They preach to the people committed to them the faith they must believe and put into practice, and by the light of the Holy Spirit they illustrate that faith. They bring forth from the treasury of Revelation new things and old, making it bear fruit and they vigilantly ward off any errors that threaten their flock. Bishops, teaching in communion with the Roman Pontiff, are to be respected by all as witnesses to divine and Catholic truth. In matters of faith and morals, the bishops speak in the name of Christ and the faithful are to accept their teaching and adhere to it with religious assent. This religious submission of mind and will must be shown in a special way to the authentic magisterium of the Roman Pontiff, even when he is not speaking ex cathedra, that is, his supreme magisterium is to be acknowledged with reverence, and the judgments issued by him must be sincerely adhered to, according to his manifest mind and will. His mind and will in the matter may be known from the character of the documents, from his frequent repetition of the same doctrine, or from his manner of speaking.

The College of Bishops Is Infallible under the Pope

Although the individual bishops do not enjoy the prerogative of infallibility, they nevertheless proclaim Christ's doctrine infallibly whenever, even though dispersed throughout the world, but still maintaining the bond of communion among themselves and with the successor of Peter, and authentically teaching matters of faith and morals, they are in agreement on one position as definitively to be held. This is even more clearly verified when, gathered together in an ecumenical council, they are teachers and judges of faith and morals for the universal Church, whose definitions must be adhered to with the submission of faith.

This Infallibility Is That of the Church

This infallibility with which the divine Redeemer willed his Church to be endowed in defining doctrine of faith and morals, is as extensive as the deposit of revelation, which must be religiously guarded and faithfully expounded. This is the infallibility which the Roman Pontiff, the head of the college of bishops, enjoys in virtue of his office, when, as the supreme shepherd and teacher of all the faithful, who confirms his brethren in their faith, by a definitive act he proclaims a doctrine of faith or morals. Therefore his definitions, of themselves, and not from the consent of the Church, are justly styled irreformable, since they are pronounced with the assistance of the Holy Spirit, promised to him in blessed Peter, and consequently they need no approval of others, nor do they allow an appeal to any other judgment. For then the Roman Pontiff is pronouncing judgment not as a private person, but as the supreme teacher of the universal Church, and in him the charism of infallibility of the Church itself is individually present, for he is expounding or defending a doctrine of Catholic faith. The infallibility promised to the Church resides also in the body of bishops, when that body exercises the supreme magisterium with the successor of Peter. To these definitions the assent of the Church can never be wanting, on account of the activity of that same Holy Spirit, by which the whole flock of Christ is preserved and progresses in unity of faith.

The Pope and Bishops Defend Revelation

When the Roman Pontiff or the body of bishops together with him defines a statement, they pronounce it in accordance with revelation itself. All are bound to abide by revelation and to conform to it. Whether it is written or orally handed down, it is transmitted in its entirety through the legitimate succession of bishops and especially by the care of the Roman Pontiff himself, and under the guiding light of the spirit of truth it is religiously preserved and faithfully expounded in the Church. The Roman Pontiff and the bishops, aware of their responsibility in so grave a matter, spare no care or effort to probe deeper by approved methods into revelation and give it apt expression; but they do not accept a new public revelation as pertaining to the divine deposit of faith.

The Church of Christ Present in Local Communities

26.   A bishop marked with the fullness of the sacrament of orders, is "the steward of the grace of the supreme priesthood," especially in the Eucharist, which he offers or causes to be offered, and by which the Church continually lives and grows. This Church of Christ is truly present in all legitimate local congregations of the faithful which, united with their pastors, are themselves called churches in the New Testament. For in their locality these are the new people

called by God, in the Holy Spirit and in much fullness. In them the faithful are gathered together by the preaching of the Gospel of Christ, and the mystery of the Lord's Supper is celebrated, "that by the food and blood of the Lord's body the whole brotherhood may be joined together" (Mozarabic Prayer). In any community of the altar, under the sacred ministry of the bishop, there is exhibited a symbol of that charity and "unity of the mystical body, without which there can be no salvation" (St. Thomas, *Summa Theol.* III). In these communities, though frequently small and poor, or living in the diaspora, Christ is present, and in virtue of his presence there is brought together one, holy, catholic and apostolic Church. For "the partaking of the body and blood of Christ does nothing other than make us be transformed into that which we consume" (St. Leo, *Serm.*).

Bishops Regulate Celebration of Eucharist

Every legitimate celebration of the Eucharist is regulated by the bishop, to whom is committed the office of offering the worship of Christian religion to the Divine Majesty and of administering it in accordance with the Lord's commandments and the Church's laws, as further defined by his particular judgment for his diocese.

The Bishops Communicate the Holiness of Christ

Bishops thus, by praying and laboring for the people, bring about a manifold and abundant outpouring from the fullness of Christ's holiness. By the ministry of the word they communicate God's power to those who believe unto salvation, and through the sacraments, the regular and fruitful distribution of which they regulate by their authority, they sanctify the faithful. They direct the conferring of baptism, by which a sharing in the kingly priesthood of Christ is granted. They are the original ministers of confirmation, dispensers of sacred orders and the moderators of penitential discipline, and they earnestly exhort and instruct their people to carry out with faith and reverence their part in the liturgy and especially in the holy sacrifice of the Mass. Lastly, by the example of their way of life they must be an influence for good to those over whom they preside, refraining from all evil and, as far as they are able with God's help, exchanging evil for good, so that together with the flock committed to their care they may arrive at eternal life.

Bishops by Their Office Are Rulers of Their Churches

27.   Bishops, as vicars and ambassadors of Christ, govern the

particular churches entrusted to them by their counsel, exhortations, example, and also by their authority and sacred power, which indeed they use only for the edification of their flock in truth and holiness, remembering that he who is greater should become as the lesser and he who is the chief become as the servant. This power, which they personally exercise in Christ's name, is proper, ordinary and immediate, although its exercise is ultimately regulated by the supreme authority of the Church, and can be circumscribed by certain limits, for the advantage of the Church or of the faithful. In virtue of this power, bishops have the sacred right and the duty before the Lord to make laws for their subjects, to pass judgment on them and to moderate everything pertaining to the ordering of worship and the apostolate.

Bishops Exercise Authority As a Right

The pastoral office or the habitual and daily care of their sheep is entrusted to them completely; they are not to be regarded as vicars of the Roman Pontiffs, for they exercise an authority that is proper to them, and are quite correctly called "prelate," heads of the people whom they govern. Their power, therefore, is not destroyed by the supreme and universal power, but on the contrary it is affirmed, strengthened and vindicated by it, since the Holy Spirit unfailingly preserves the form of government established by Christ the Lord in his Church.

Care of a Bishop for His Flock

A bishop, since he is sent by the Father to govern his family, must keep before his eyes the example of the Good Shepherd, who came not to be ministered unto but to minister, and to lay down his life for his sheep. Being taken from among men, and himself beset with weakness, he is able to have compassion on the ignorant and erring. Let him not refuse to listen to his subjects, whom he cherishes as his true sons and exhorts to cooperate readily with him. As having one day to render an account for their souls, he takes care of them by his prayer, preaching, and every work of charity, but he is also solicitous of those who are not yet of the one flock, who are commended to him in the Lord. Since, like Paul the Apostle, he is debtor to all men, let him be ready to preach the Gospel to all, and to urge his faithful to apostolic and missionary activity. The faithful likewise must cling to their bishop, as the Church does to Christ, and Jesus Christ to the Father, so that all may be of one mind through unity, and abound to the glory of God.

The Bishops Share Their Ministry with the Priests

28.   Christ, whom the Father has sanctified and sent into the
world, has through his apostles, made their successors, the bishops,
partakers of his consecration and his mission. They have legitimately
handed on to different individuals in the Church various degrees of
participation in this ministry. Thus the divinely established ecclesiastical ministry is exercised on different levels by those who from
antiquity have been called bishops, priests and deacons. Priests,
although they do not possess the highest degree of the priesthood,
and although they are dependent on the bishops in the exercise of
their power, are nevertheless united with the bishops in sacerdotal
dignity. By the power of the sacrament of orders, in the image of
Christ the eternal high priest, they are consecrated to preach the
Gospel and shepherd the faithful and to celebrate divine worship,
so that they are true priests of the New Testament. Partakers of the
function of Christ the sole mediator, on their level of ministry, they
announce the divine word to all. They exercise their sacred function
especially in the eucharistic worship or the celebration of the Mass
by which, acting in the person of Christ and proclaiming his mystery, they unite the prayers of the faithful with the sacrifice of their
head and renew and apply in the sacrifice of the Mass until the
coming of the Lord the only sacrifice of the New Testament, namely,
that of Christ offering himself once for all a spotless victim to the
Father. For the sick and sinners among the faithful, they exercise
the ministry of alleviation and reconciliation and they present the
needs and the prayers of the faithful to God the Father. Exercising
within the limits of their authority the function of Christ as shepherd and head, they gather together God's family as a brotherhood
all of one mind, and lead them in the Spirit, through Christ, to
God the Father. In the midst of the flock they adore him in spirit
and in truth. Finally, they labor in word and doctrine, believing
what they have read and pondered in the law of God, teaching what
they have believed, and putting in practice what they have taught.

Priests Form One Priesthood with Their Bishop

Priests, prudent cooperators with the episcopal order, its aid and
instrument, called to serve the people of God, constitute one priesthood with their bishop although bound by a diversity of duties. Asso-
ciated with their bishop in a spirit of trust and generosity, they make
him present in a certain sense in the individual local congregations,
and take upon themselves, as far as they are able, his duties and

burden of his care, and daily discharge them with zeal. As they sanctify and govern under the bishop's authority, that part of the Lord's
flock entrusted to them, they make the universal Church visible in
their own locality and bring an efficacious assistance to the building
up of the whole body of Christ. Intent always upon the welfare of
God's children, they must strive to lend their effort to the pastoral
work of the whole diocese, and even of the entire Church. On
account of this sharing in their priesthood and mission, let priests
sincerely look upon the bishop as their father and reverently obey
him. And let the bishop regard his priests as his co-workers and as
sons and friends, just as Christ called his disciples no longer servants
but friends. All priests, both diocesan and religious, by reason of
orders and ministry, fit into this body of bishops and priests, and
serve the good of the whole Church according to their vocation and
the grace given to them.

The Brotherhood of the Priesthood

In virtue of their common sacred ordination and mission, all
priests are bound together in intimate brotherhood, which naturally
and freely manifests itself in mutual aid, spiritual as well as material, pastoral as well as personal, in their meetings and in communion of life, of labor and charity.

Priests, An Example to Their Flock

Let them, as fathers in Christ, take care of the faithful whom they
have begotten by baptism and their teaching. Becoming from the
heart a pattern to the flock, let them so lead and serve their local
community that it may worthily be called by that name, by which
the one and entire people of God is signed, namely, the Church of
God. Let them remember that by their daily life and zeal they must
present an image of a truly sacerdotal and pastoral ministry to the
faithful and the unbelievers, to Catholics and non-Catholics, and
that to all they bear witness to the truth and life, and as good shepherds seek those also, who though baptized in the Catholic Church
have fallen away from the use of the sacraments, or even from the
faith.

Priests Work for the Unity of Mankind

Because the human race today is becoming more and more a civic,
economic and social unity, it is the more necessary that priests, by
combining their resources under the leadership of the bishops and
the Supreme Pontiff, should eliminate everything that separates, so

that the whole human race may be brought into the unity of the family of God.

Deacons

29.   At a lower level of the hierarchy are deacons, upon whom hands are imposed "not unto the priesthood, but unto a ministry of service." Strengthened by sacramental grace, in communion with the bishop and his group of priests, they serve in the diaconate of the liturgy, of the word, and of charity to the people of God. It is the duty of the deacon, according as it is assigned to him by competent authority, to administer solemn baptism, to be custodian and dispenser of the Eucharist, to assist at and bless marriages in the name of the Church, to bring Viaticum to the dying, to read the Sacred Scripture to the faithful, to instruct and exhort the people, to preside over the worship and prayer of the faithful, to administer sacramentals, to officiate at funeral and burial services. Dedicated to duties of charity and of administration, let deacons be mindful of the admonition of Blessed Polycarp: "Be merciful, diligent, walking according to the truth of the Lord, who became the servant of all."

Since these duties, so very necessary to the life of the Church, can be fulfilled only with difficulty in many regions within the discipline of the Latin Church as it exists today, the diaconate can in the future be restored as a proper and permanent rank of the hierarchy. It pertains to the various competent territorial bodies of bishops, with the approval of the Supreme Pontiff, to decide whether and where it is opportune for such deacons to be established for the care of souls. With the consent of the Roman Pontiff, this diaconate can, in the future, be conferred upon men of more mature age, even upon those living in the married state. It may be conferred upon suitable young men, for whom the law of celibacy must remain intact.

For every layman Chapter IV is one of the most important statements in this great document. Here we have, for the first time, an official pronouncement by the Church on the position and duties of the laity in the Church.

By the laity is meant all men and women who have not received holy orders or consecration in religious life.

For a lay retreatant there is a wealth of material contained herein for prayerful thought during the retreat and thereafter. In reading this chapter one should note especially the following points and try to relate them to himself:

a. Everything already said about the people of God applies to the laity as well as to religious and clergy. They too, share in the mission of the Church, being members of the people of God.

b. The laity strive for holiness in the secular life they live, working to sanctify the world from within, by engaging in temporal affairs and ordering them according to the plan of God.

c. They share the dignity of baptism with the pope, bishops and clergy.

d. The different functions of bishops, clergy and laity make for the unity of the one body of Christ, for they are all united in charity, which they all exercise in common. They are all brothers of the same brother, who is Christ.

e. Every layman is bound to be apostolic by virtue of his baptism, for everyone is called to take part in the mission of the Church.

f. The layman is motivated and urged by charity, which is communicated to him through the sacraments, and especially by the Holy Eucharist.

g. Certain laymen are invited by the hierarchy to share directly in the apostolate of the hierarchy.

h. The layman shares through baptism in the priestly office of Christ, by his dedication to Christ, his confirmation by the Holy Spirit, his worship, his sacrifices and his work.

i. He shares also in the prophetic office of Christ by his discernment of faith and by giving witness to Christ in the world. In regards to this point the Constitution lays great stress on family life.

j. Besides helping to evangelize the world for Christ, the laity also help make it a better place in which to live. This is the way they share in the royal office of Christ who established his kingdom to be fulfilled in justice, truth, love and peace.

k. The layman, though he must distinguish between his duties as a citizen of this world and as a member of the Church, must judge and act with a single conscience, formed in the light of Christ's teaching.

l. The laity, in relation to the clergy, have a right to the spiritual goods of the Church, especially the Word of God and the sacraments. They have a right to express their opinion in what concerns the good of the Church. The laity, on the other hand, have the duty to obey their rulers and teachers in the Church.

The chapter ends by strongly exhorting bishops and clergy to have confidence in the laity and to assign them work in the service of the Church, leaving them room for the exercise of initiative and freedom. This type of relationship should make for union between clergy and people, which, in turn, will help the Church fulfill its mission.

Chapter IV

THE LAITY

30.   Having set forth the functions of the hierarchy, the Sacred Council gladly turns its attention to the state of those faithful called the laity. Everything that has been said above concerning the people of God is intended for the laity, religious and clergy alike. But there are certain things which pertain in a special way to the laity, both men and women, by reason of their situation and mission. Owing to the special circumstances of our time, the foundations of this doctrine must be more thoroughly examined. Their bishops know how much the laity contribute to the welfare of the entire Church. The bishops also know that they themselves were not ordained by Christ to undertake alone the entire salvific mission of the Church toward the world. On the contrary, they understand that it is their noble duty to shepherd the faithful and to recognize their ministeries and charisms, so that all according to their proper role may cooperate with one mind in this common undertaking. For we must all "practice the truth in love, and so grow up in all things in him who is head, Christ. For from him the whole body, being closely joined and knit together through every joint of the system, according to the functioning in due measure of each single part, derives its increase to the building up of itself in love" (Eph 4:15–16).

Who Are the Laity?

31.   The term laity is here understood to mean all the faithful except those in holy orders and those in the state of religious life especially approved by the Church. The faithful laity are by baptism made one body with Christ and are constituted among the people of God; they are in their own way made sharers in the priestly, prophetical, and kingly office of Christ; and they carry out in their own way the mission of the whole Christian people in the Church and in the world.

The Specific Task of the Laity

What specifically characterizes the laity is their secular nature. It is true that those in holy orders can at times be engaged in secular activities, and even have a secular profession. But they are by reason of their particular vocation especially and professedly ordained to the sacred ministry. Similarly, by their state in life, religious give splendid and striking testimony that the world cannot be transformed and offered to God without the spirit of the beatitudes. But the laity, by their very vocation, seek the kingdom of God by engaging in temporal affairs and by ordering them according to the plan of God. They live in the world, that is, in every secular profession and occupation. They live in the ordinary circumstances of family and social life, from which the very web of their existence is woven. They are called there by God that exercising their proper function, and led by the spirit of the Gospel, they may work for the sanctification of the world from within as a leaven. In this way they make Christ known to others, especially by the testimony of a life that shines with faith, hope and charity. Therefore, since they are involved in temporal affairs of every kind, it is their special task to bring order and to shed light upon them that they may be transformed and may increasingly develop according to Christ to the praise of the Creator and the Redeemer.

All in the Church Have a Common Dignity

32.   By divine institution Holy Church is ordered and governed with wonderful diversity. "For just as in one body we have many members, yet all the members have not the same function, so we, the many, are one body in Christ, but severally members one of another" (Rom 12:4–5). Therefore, the chosen people of God is one: "One Lord, one faith, one baptism" (Eph 4:5); sharing a common dignity as members from their regeneration in Christ; having the same filial grace and the same vocation to perfection; possessing in

common one salvation, one hope and one undivided charity. There
is, therefore, in Christ and in the Church no inequality on the basis
of race or nationality, social condition or sex, because "there is neither Jew nor Greek; there is neither bond nor free; there is neither
male nor female. For you are all 'one' in Christ Jesus" (Gal 3:28;
See Col 3:11).

Diversity of Duties for the Sake of Union

If therefore in the Church everyone does not proceed by the same
path, nevertheless all are called to sanctity and have received an
equal privilege of faith through the justice of God. If by the will of
Christ some are made teachers, pastors and dispensers of mysteries
on behalf of others, yet all share a true equality with regard to the
dignity and to the activity common to all the faithful for the building up of the body of Christ. For the distinction which the Lord
made between sacred ministers and the rest of the people of God
bears within it a certain union, since bishops and the other faithful
are bound to each other by a mutual need. Bishops of the Church,
following the example of the Lord, should minister to one another
and to the other faithful. These in their turn should not hesitate to
lend their united assistance to their bishops and teachers. Thus in
their diversity all bear witness to the wonderful unity in the body
of Christ. This very diversity of graces, ministries and works gathers
the children of God into one, because "all these things are the work
of one and the same Spirit" (1 Cor 12:11).

Union of Clergy and the Laity

Therefore, through the kindness of God the laity have Christ for
their brother, and though he is the Lord of all, he came not to be
served but to serve. They also have for their brothers those in the
sacred ministry who by teaching, by sanctifying and by ruling with
the authority of Christ feed the family of God so that the new commandment of charity may be fulfilled by all. St. Augustine puts this
very beautifully when he says: "What I am for you terrifies me;
what I am with you consoles me. For you I am a bishop; but with
you I am a Christian. The former is a duty; the latter a grace. The
former is a danger; the latter salvation" (Serm. 340).

The Laity Must Be Active

33.   The laity are gathered together in the people of God and
make up the body of Christ under one head. All without exception
are called upon, as living members, to expend all their energy for

the growth of the Church and its continuous sanctification, since this very energy is a gift of the Creator and a blessing of the Redeemer.

The Meaning of the Lay Apostolate

The lay apostolate, is a participation in the salvific mission of the Church itself. Through their baptism and confirmation all are commissioned to that apostolate by the Lord himself. Moreover, by the sacraments, especially Holy Eucharist, that charity toward God and man which is the soul of the apostolate is communicated and nourished. Now the laity are called in a special way to make the Church present and operative in those places and circumstances where only through them can it become the salt of the earth. Thus every layman, in virtue of the very gifts bestowed upon him, is at the same time a witness and a living instrument of the mission of the Church itself "according to the measure of Christ's bestowal" (Eph 4:7).

Specialized Assignments by the Hierarchy

Besides this apostolate which certainly pertains to all Christians, the laity can also be called in various ways to a more direct form of cooperation in the apostolate of the hierarchy. This was the way certain men and women assisted Paul the Apostle in the Gospel, laboring much in the Lord. Further, they have the capacity to be used by the hierarchy for certain ecclesiastical duties which have a spiritual objective.

Laymen To Be Given Opportunities

Upon all the laity, therefore, rests the noble duty of working to extend the divine plan of salvation to all men in every age and in every land. Consequently, every opportunity should be given them so that, according to their abilities and the needs of the times, they may zealously participate in the saving work of the Church.

Christ the Priest Urges the Laity

34.   The supreme and eternal priest, Christ Jesus, since he wills to continue his witness and service through the laity also, vivifies them in his Spirit and increasingly urges them on to every good and perfect work.

The Laity Share in Christ's Priestly Office

Besides intimately linking them to his life and his mission, he also gives to the laity a sharing in his priestly function of offering spiritual worship for the glory of God and the salvation of men. For this reason the laity, dedicated to Christ and anointed by the Holy Spirit, are wonderfully called and prepared so that ever more abundant fruits of the Spirit may be produced in them. For all their works, prayers and apostolic endeavors, their ordinary married and family life, their daily occupations, their physical and mental relaxation, if carried out in the Holy Spirit, and even the hardships of life, if patiently borne—all these become "spiritual sacrifices acceptable to God through Jesus Christ" (1 Pet 2:5). Together with the offering of the Lord's body, these sacrifices are most fittingly offered in the celebration of the Eucharist. Thus, the laity also, by the adoration of their holy living in every place consecrate the world itself to God.

The Laity Share in Christ's Prophetic Office

35.   Christ, the great prophet, who proclaimed the kingdom of his Father, both by the testimony of his life and the power of his words, continually fulfills his prophetic office until the complete manifestation of glory. He does this not only through the hierarchy who teach in his name and with his authority; but also through the laity whom he therefore establishes as his witnesses and teaches by discernment of the faith and the grace of the word, so that the power of the Gospel may shine forth in their daily social and family life. They show themselves as children of the promise, and thus strong in faith and in hope they make the most of the present, and with patience await the glory that is to come. Let them not hide this hope in their inmost heart, but even in the program of their secular life let them express it by a continual conversion and by wrestling "against the world-rulers of this darkness, against the spiritual forces of wickedness" (Eph 6:12).

The Living Witness of the Laity

Just as the sacraments of the New Law, by which the life and the apostolate of the faithful are nourished, prefigure a new heaven and a new earth, so too the laity go forth as powerful proclaimers of a faith in things to be hoped for, when they courageously join to their profession of faith a life rooted in faith. This evangelization, that is, the announcing of Christ by a living testimony as well as by the spoken word, takes on a specific quality and a special force in that it is carried out in the ordinary surroundings of the world.

The Prophetic Office of the Family

In the exercise of this the prophetic function, that state of life which is sanctified by a special sacrament is obviously of great importance, namely, married and family life. The family, when the Christian religion pervades the whole way of life and gradually transforms it, is an excellent training ground for the lay apostolate and provides ample opportunity to exercise it. In the family husbands and wives find their proper vocation as witnesses of the faith and love of Christ to one another and to their children. The Christian family loudly proclaims both the present virtues of the kingdom of God and the hope of a blessed life to come. Thus by its example and its witness it accuses the world of sin and enlightens those who seek the truth.

The Laity and the Evangelization of the World

Consequently, even when preoccupied with temporal cares, the laity can and must perform a work of great value for the evangelization of the world. When there are no sacred ministers, or when the clergy are impeded from the exercise of their duties in time of persecution, laymen have to perform some of the sacred functions as best they can. Many laymen devote all their energies to apostolic work, but every layman must cooperate in the external spread and the dynamic growth of the kingdom of Christ in the world. Therefore, let the laity seriously strive to acquire a more profound grasp of revealed truth, and let them insistently beg of God the gift of wisdom.

The Laity Prepare the Kingdom of Christ

36.   Christ, becoming obedient even unto death and for this reason exalted by the Father, entered into the glory of his kingdom. To him all things are made subject until he subjects himself and all created things to the Father that God may be all in all. Now Christ has communicated this royal power to his disciples that they may be constituted in royal freedom and that by true penance and a holy life they may conquer the reign of sin in themselves. Further, he has shared this power so that serving Christ in their fellowmen they may by humility and patience lead their brethren to that king to serve whom is to reign. For the Lord wishes to spread his kingdom also by means of the faithful, namely, a kingdom of truth and life, a kingdom of holiness and grace, a kingdom of justice, love and peace. In this kingdom creation itself will be delivered from its slavery to corruption into the freedom of the glory of the sons of God. Clearly then a great promise and a great trust is committed to the disciples: "All things are yours, and you are Christ's, and Christ is God's" (1 Cor 3:23).

The Laity and God's Plan for the World

The faithful, therefore, must recognize the inner nature of the whole of creation, its value, its orientation to the praise of God. They must assist each other to live holier lives even by means of their secular occupations. In this way the world will be permeated by the spirit of Christ and it will more effectively fulfill its purpose in justice, charity and peace. The laity have the principal role in the overall fulfillment of this duty. Therefore, by their competence in secular training and by their activity, elevated from within by the grace of Christ, they should do all they can to perfect the works of creation by human labor, technical skill and the resources of civilization for the benefit of all men according to the design of the Creator and the light of his Word. The goods of this world should be more equitably distributed among all men, and in their own way be conducive to universal progress in human and Christian freedom. In this manner, through the members of the Church, Christ will illumine progressively the whole of human society with his saving light.

The Laity Prepare the World for Christ's Message

Moreover, let the laity singly and by their combined efforts remedy the practices and conditions of the world, insofar as they are an inducement to sin, so that they all may be conformed to the norms of justice and may favor the practice of virtue rather than hinder it. By so doing they will permeate culture and human activity with genuine moral values; they will better prepare the field of the world for the seed of the Word of God; and at the same time they will open wider the doors of the Church by which the message of peace may enter the world.

The Laity as Christians and as Citizens

The economy of salvation demands that the faithful should learn to distinguish carefully between those rights and duties which are theirs as members of the Church, and those which they have as members of human society. Let them strive to reconcile the two, remembering that in every temporal affair they must be guided by a Christian conscience, since even in secular business there is no human activity which can be withdrawn from God's dominion. In our own time, moreover, it is most urgent that this distinction and also this harmony should shine forth more clearly than ever in the lives of the faithful, so that the mission of the Church may correspond more fully to the special conditions of the world today. It must be recognized that the temporal sphere is governed by its own principles, since it is rightly concerned with the interests of this world. But that ominous doctrine which attempts to build a society with no regard whatever for religion and which attacks and destroys the religious liberty of its citizens is rightly to be rejected.

The Rights of the Laity in the Church

37.   The laity have the right, like all Christians, to receive in abundance from their spiritual shepherds the spiritual goods of the Church, especially the assistance of the Word of God and of the sacraments. They should frankly reveal to them their needs and desires with freedom and that confidence which the children of God and brothers in Christ should have for one another. They are, by reason of their knowledge, competence or ability permitted and sometimes even obliged to express their opinion on those things which concern the good of the Church. When occasion arises, let this be done through the channels established by the Church for this purpose. Let it always be done in truth, in courage and in prudence, with reverence and charity toward those who by reason of their sacred office represent the person of Christ.

The Laity Owe Obedience to Their Spiritual Shepherds

The laity should, like all Christians, promptly accept in Christian obedience decisions of their bishops, since they are representatives of Christ as well as teachers and rulers in the Church. Let them follow the example of Christ, who by his obedience even unto death, opened to all men the blessed way of the liberty of the children of God. Nor should they omit to pray for those placed over them, for they keep watch as having to render an account of their souls, so that they may do this with joy and not with grief.

Bishops Should Promote Confidence in the Laity

Let the bishops recognize and promote the dignity as well as the responsibility of the laity in the Church. Let them willingly make use of their prudent advice. Let them confidently assign duties to them in the service of the Church, allowing them freedom and room for action. Further, let them encourage lay people so that they may undertake tasks on their own initiative. Let them consider attentively in Christ and with fatherly love the projects, suggestions and desires proposed by the laity. However, let the bishops carefully recognize that just freedom to which everyone has the right in the earthly city.

Hopes from Cooperation of Laity and Bishops

A great many wonderful things are to be hoped for from this familiar dialogue between the laity and their bishops: in the laity a strengthened sense of personal responsibility; a renewed enthusiasm; a more ready application of their talents to the projects of their bishops. The latter, on the other hand, aided by the experience of the laity, can more clearly and more efficiently come to decisions regarding both spiritual and temporal matters. In this way the whole Church, strengthened by each one of its members will more effectively fulfill its mission for the life of the world.

Each Layman is a Witness

38.   Each individual layman must stand before the world as a witness to the resurrection and life of the Lord Jesus and as a sign of the living God. All the laity as a community and each one according to his ability must nourish the world with spiritual fruits. They must spread in the world that spirit which animates the poor, the meek, the peacemakers—whom the Lord in the Gospel proclaimed as blessed. In a word, "Christians must be to the world what the soul is to the body" (*Epist. ad Diognetum*).

Introductory Note   Chapter V

After Chapter IV this next chapter is of vital importance to all, for it details for us the call of God to everyone to be holy, and describes the ways and means such holiness is to be attained.

The holiness of the Church stems from the holiness of the Blessed Trinity. Christ loves the Church as his bride. He delivered himself up for her and makes her holy by the gift of the Holy Spirit as his mystical body. All the members of the Church are therefore called to one and the same holiness, which must be made manifest to the world.

It is baptism and the gift of the Holy Spirit which are the foundation of this holiness. It is expressed in the love of God and of neighbor and is shown in the following of Christ in his poverty and suffering.

The chapter goes on to speak about the attainment of holiness through the perfect performance of the duties that belong to the various ways of life in the Church.

Bishops and priests find their holiness in the exercise of their office. They are given special graces for their responsibilities. A special paragraph is devoted to the holiness of married couples; another passage to the holiness to be derived from work; and yet another to the holiness rooted in suffering.

The necessity of prayer, the study of the Word of God and the use of the sacraments are shown as necessary for the increase of charity, which is the fulfillment of the law. This charity requires that we be ready to confess Christ before men, even in times of persecution. The chapter concludes with a statement on the sanctity of a life of chastity and of the religious state. Even though all cannot practice the counsels of perfection, they must not become too attached to the things of this world while they seek perfection in their own state of life.

Chapter V

THE UNIVERSAL CALL
TO HOLINESS

39.   The Church, whose mystery is being set forth by this Sacred Synod, is held to be indefectibly holy. Indeed, Christ, the Son of God, who with the Father and the Spirit is praised as "uniquely holy" (Roman Missal), loved the Church as his bride, delivering himself up for her. He did this that he might sanctify her. He united her to himself as his own body and crowned her with the gift of the Holy Spirit for God's glory. Therefore in the Church, everyone whether belonging to the hierarchy, or under its pastoral care, is called to holiness according to the saying of the Apostle: "For this is the will of God, your sanctification" (1 Thess 4:3; Eph 1:4). However, this holiness of the Church is unceasingly manifested, and must be manifested, in the fruits of grace which the Spirit produces in the faithful; it is expressed in many ways in individuals, who in their walk of life, strive toward the perfection of charity and thus are an inspiration to others. In a very special way this holiness appears in the practice of the counsels, customarily called "evangelical." This practice of the counsels, under the impulsion of the Holy Spirit, undertaken by many Christians, either privately or in a situation or state of life approved by the Church, gives to the world, as indeed it ought, an outstanding witness and example of this same holiness.

Baptism—the Foundation of Holiness

40.   The Lord Jesus, the divine teacher and model of all perfection, preached holiness of life to each and everyone of his disciples of every condition. It is he who initiates and perfects this holiness of life: "Be you therefore perfect, even as your heavenly Father is perfect" (Matt 5:48). Indeed he sent the Holy Spirit upon all men that he might move them from within to love God with their whole heart and their whole soul, with all their mind and all their strength and that they might love each other as Christ loves them. The followers of Christ are called by God, not because of their works, but according to his own purpose and grace. They are justified in the Lord Jesus, because in the baptism of faith they truly become sons of God and sharers in the divine nature. In very deed they have been made holy. The holiness they have received by God's gift they must retain and complete in their lives. They are warned by the Apostle to live "as becomes saints" (Eph 5:3), and to put on "as God's chosen ones, holy and beloved, a heart of mercy, kindness, humility, meekness, patience" (Col 3:12), and to possess the fruit of the Spirit in holiess. Since truly we all offend in many things we all need God's mercies continually and we all must daily pray: "Forgive us our debts" (Matt 6:12).

All the Faithful Are Called to Holiness

Thus it is evident to everyone, that all the faithful of Christ of whatever state or human condition, are called to the fullness of the Christian life and to the perfection of charity. Even society on earth is made more genuinely human by holiness. To reach this perfection the faithful must use all their energy which they have received as a gift from Christ so that they may follow in his footsteps and conform themselves to his image seeking the will of the Father in all things. They must devote themselves with all their being to the glory of God and the service of their neighbor. In this way, the holiness of the people of God will grow into an abundant harvest of good, as is admirably shown by the life of so many saints in Church history.

Holiness Is the Following of Christ

41.   In the various walks of life with their differing duties, one and the same holiness is cultivated by all who are moved by the Spirit of God, and who obey the voice of the Father and worship God the Father in spirit and in truth. They follow the poor Christ, the humble and cross-bearing Christ in order to earn a share in his

glory. Everyone, according to his personal gifts and duties, must walk unhesitatingly in the path of living faith, which arouses hope, and works through charity.

Bishops Derive Holiness from Their Ministry

In the first place, the bishops of Christ's flock must be holy, eager, humble and courageous in carrying out their ministry, in imitation of the eternal high priest, the shepherd and guardian of our souls. They ought to fulfill this duty in such a way that it will be the principal means also of their own sanctification. Those chosen for the fullness of the priesthood are endowed with sacramental grace that they may perfectly exercise their duty of pastoral charity in every aspect of episcopal care and service, in prayer, sacrifice and preaching. This same sacramental grace, gives them the courage necessary to lay down their lives for their sheep, and enables them to bring about greater holiness in the Church by their daily example, having become a pattern for their flock.

The Same Is True of Priests

Priests form the spiritual crown of the bishops and participate in the grace of their office. Following the example of the episcopal order they should grow daily in love of God and of their neighbor by the exercise of their office through Christ, the eternal and one mediator. They should preserve the bond of priestly communion, and they should abound in every spiritual good and thus present to all men a living witness to God. All this they should do in emulation of those priests who often, in the course of centuries, have left an outstanding example of the holiness of humble and hidden service. Their praise lives on in the Church of God. By their very office of praying and offering sacrifice for their own people and the entire people of God, they should rise to greater holiness. Keeping in mind what they are doing and imitating what they are handling, priests, far from allowing the responsibilities, risks and anxieties of their apostolic life to be an obstacle, should by these means rise to greater holiness, to the comfort of the whole Church of God. This is not possible unless they feed and strengthen their life with frequent meditation. All priests, and especially those who from the special title of their ordination, are called "diocesan priests," should keep continually before their minds the fact that their loyalty to their bishop and generous cooperation with him are of the greatest value in their growth in holiness.

Deacons and Others

Ministers of lesser rank are also sharers in the mission and grace of the supreme priest. In the first place among these ministers are deacons, who, in as much as they are dispensers of Christ's mysteries and servants of the Church, should keep themselves free from every vice, be pleasing to God and be an example of all virtue before men. Clerics, who are called by the Lord and are set aside as his portion in order to prepare themselves for the various ministerial offices under the watchful eye of the bishops, have a duty to bring their hearts and minds into conformity with this noble calling. They will accomplish this by their constancy in prayer, by their fervent love, and by bearing in mind whatever is true, just and of good repute. They will accomplish all this for the glory and honor of God. The same is true of those laymen, chosen of God and called by the bishop to spend themselves completely in apostolic labors, working the Lord's field with much success.

Holiness of Married Couples

Furthermore, married couples and Christian parents should follow their own proper path to holiness by faithful love. They should sustain one another in grace throughout their married lives. They should instill in their offspring, which they lovingly welcome as God's gift, Christian doctrine and the evangelical virtues. In this manner, they offer all men the example of unwearying and generous love; in this way they build up the brotherhood of charity; in so doing, they stand as the witnesses and cooperators in the fruitfulness of Holy Mother Church; by such lives, they are a sign and a participation in the very love, with which Christ loved his bride and for which he delivered himself up for her. A like example, given in a different way, is that offered by widows and single people, who make great contributions toward holiness and apostolic endeavor in the Church.

Holiness of Work

Finally, those who engage in labor, frequently of a heavy nature, should perfect themselves by their human work. They should help their fellow citizens, and raise all society, and even creation itself, to a better mode of existence. Indeed, they should imitate by their lively charity, their joyous hope and their voluntary sharing of each others' burdens, the very Christ whose hands used carpenter's tools and who in union with his Father, is continually working for the salvation of all men. By means of their daily work, they should climb to the heights of holiness, which is indeed apostolic.

Holiness of the Afflicted

May all those who are weighed down with poverty, infirmity and sickness, as well as those who bear various hardships or suffer persecution for justice sake, know they are united with the suffering Christ in a special way for the salvation of the world. The Lord called them blessed in his Gospel and they are those whom "the God of all graces, who has called us unto his eternal glory in Christ Jesus, will himself, after we have suffered a little while, perfect, strengthen and establish" (1 Pet 5:10).

Abandonment to Divine Providence

All the faithful, therefore, will be sanctified daily more and more in and by the situations, duties and circumstances of their lives. These things will be the means of their advance in holiness if they accept everything from the hands of the Heavenly Father with faith, and if they cooperate with the divine will, manifesting to all men in the very service of their lives, the charity with which God has loved the world.

Charity

42.   "God is love, and he who abides in love, abides in God, and God in him" (1 John 4:16). God pours out his love into our hearts through the Holy Spirit, who has been given to us; thus the first and most necessary gift is charity by which we love God above all things and our neighbor because of God. Indeed, in order that charity may grow as a good seed and bring forth fruit in the soul, each one of the faithful must willingly listen to the Word of God, and with his grace fulfill his will, by actions. This includes the use of the sacraments and in a special way the Eucharist, the frequent participation in the sacred action of the liturgy, application to prayer, self-abnegation, active fraternal service and the constant use of all the virtues. For charity, as the bond of perfection and the fullness of the law, rules over all the means of attaining holiness and gives them life and guides us to our objectives. It is the love of God and the love of one's neighbor which points out the true disciple of Christ.

All Must Be Willing to Profess Christ

Since Jesus, the Son of God, manifested his charity by laying down his life for us, so too no one has greater love than he who lays down his life for Christ and his brothers. From earliest times, some Christians have been called upon to give the supreme testimony of this love to all men, but especially to persecutors, and this is true of every age. The Church, then, considers martyrdom as an exceptional gift and as the fullest proof of love. By martyrdom a disciple is transformed into an image of his master and is made like to him in the shedding of his blood by freely accepting death for the salvation of the world. Though few receive such an opportunity, nevertheless all must be prepared to confess Christ before men and follow him in the way of the cross, under persecution, which will never be lacking in the Church.

Chastity An Honorable State

The holiness of the Church is also fostered in a special way by the observance of the counsels proposed in the Gospel by our Lord to his disciples. An eminent position among these is held by virginity or the celibate state. This is a precious gift of divine grace given by the Father to certain souls, to enable them to devote themselves to God alone the more easily, with an undivided heart. This perfect continency, for the sake of the kingdom of heaven, has always been held in particular honor in the Church as a sign and stimulus of charity. It is a special and fruitful source of spiritual life in the world.

Sanctity of the Religious State

The Church recalls the admonition of the Apostle calling the faithful to charity where he exhorts them to experience personally what Christ Jesus had known within himself, for he "emptied himself, taking the nature of a slave . . . becoming obedient to death" (Phil 2:7–8) and because of us "being rich, he became poor" (2 Cor 8:9). Because the disciples must at all times provide an imitation and a witness of the charity and humility of Christ, Mother Church rejoices at finding within her bosom so many men and women who show forth the Savior's self-abasement by following it more closely. They profess poverty in the liberty of the sons of God and renounce their own wills. In their pursuit of perfection they do more than is required by the commandments; they submit themselves to man for God's sake, in order to follow more closely the obedient Christ.

Every State of Life Calls for Perfection

All the faithful then have an invitation which they may not refuse to the pursuit of holiness and perfection in their state of life. They must control their desires lest the use of earthly things and an attachment to riches contrary to the evangelical spirit of poverty should impede their quest for perfect charity. Let them heed the admonition of the Apostle to those who use this world; let them not come to terms with this world; for this world, as we see it, is passing away.

Introductory Note   Chapter VI

This chapter has both an importance and an interest to the laymen because for the first time it clarifies a common misunderstanding that has been noticed in the Church for years. It is important that everyone understand the religious vocation. It is of interest to the laity to see this vocation in its proper perspective in relation to his own as a layman.

Chapter VI makes it quite clear that our Lord himself established the practice of the three evangelical virtues of poverty, chastity and obedience as a definite means of striving for holiness. He not only practiced them in his own life but passed them on to his Church. The apostles and Fathers of the Church commended them even further.

Having their origin in our Lord, these virtues were taken by the Church, under the inspiration of the Holy Spirit, interpreted, their practice regulated, and a way of life was based upon them. It is a way of life that is life-long and stable.

The religious life is not an intermediate state between the clerical and lay states. In fact it is from the ranks of both the clergy and the laity that Religious are drawn to witness in their particular way to Christ and to aid in His salvific mission. This they do by active work and by prayer.

Religious men and women have an outstanding influence in stimulating love for God and for neighbor, and they show forth the life of Christ in their various activities.

Religious, in spite of their detachment from the world, are not stunted thereby in their personalities but are enriched as persons and their contribution is great in building the earthly city in accord with God's plan for his kingdom on earth.

Chapter VI

THE RELIGIOUS LIFE

43.   The evangelical counsels of chastity dedicated to God, of poverty and of obedience are based upon the words and example of the Lord. They were further commended by the apostles and Fathers, as well as by the doctors and pastors of the Church. The counsels are a divine gift, which the Church received from its Lord and which it always safeguards with the help of his grace. Church authority has the duty, under the inspiration of the Holy Spirit, of interpreting these evangelical counsels, of regulating their practice and finally of building on them stable forms of living. Thus it has come about, that from a tree which has grown in the field of the Lord, various forms of solitary and community life, as well as various religious families have branched out in a marvelous and multiple way from this divinely given seed. Thus are increased the resources for the improvement of the members and the welfare of the entire body of Christ. These religious families give their members the support of greater stability in their way of life, a proven doctrine for attaining perfection, a fraternal fellowship in the militia of Christ, and freedom strengthened by obedience. Thus men and women can fulfill their religious profession faithfully and so spiritually rejoicing make progress on the road of charity.

Religious Life Is for Clerics and Laymen

From the point of view of the divine and hierarchical structure of the Church, the religious state of life is not an intermediate state between the clerical and lay states. Rather, the faithful of Christ are called by God from both these states of life that they may enjoy this particular gift in the life of the Church and thus each in his own way, be of help to the salvific mission of the Church.

Religious Life Is a Consecration

44.   The Christian binds himself to the three counsels mentioned above either by vows, or by other sacred bonds, which in their effect are like vows, and he is totally dedicated to God whom he loves without limit, in such a way that he is related to the service of God and his honor by a new and special title. Through baptism he is indeed dead to sin and is dedicated to God, but in order that he may derive a greater fruit from the grace of his baptism, he seeks by the profession of the evangelical counsels in the Church to be freed from those obstacles, which might draw him away from the fervor of charity and the perfection of divine worship. By his profession of the evangelical counsels, then, he is more intimately consecrated to the divine service. This consecration will be the more perfect, the more the strength and stability of the bonds represent the indissoluble bond between Christ and his bride, the Church.

Religious Life Related to the Whole Church

The evangelical counsels which lead to charity join their followers to the Church and its mystery in a special way. Since this is so, their spiritual life should be devoted to the welfare of the whole Church. Hence arises their duty of working to implant and strengthen the kingdom of Christ in souls and to extend that kingdom to every clime. This duty is to be undertaken to the extent of their capacities and in keeping with the vocation they have embraced. This can be realized through prayer or active works of the apostolate. It is for this reason that the Church preserves and fosters the special character of her various religious institutes.

The Religious Life—Witness to the Kingdom of God

The profession of the evangelical counsels, then, appears as a sign which can and ought to attract all the members of the Church to an effective and prompt fulfillment of the duties of their Christian vocation. The people of God have no lasting city here below, but look forward to one that is to come. Hence, the religious state, whose purpose is to free its members from earthly cares, manifests to all believers the presence of heavenly gifts already possessed here below; it not only witnesses to the fact of a new and eternal life acquired by the redemption of Christ but also foretells the future resurrection and the glory of the heavenly kingdom. That form of life which the Son of God accepted when he came into the world to do the will of his Father, and which he suggested to his disciples who follow him, is more closely imitated and forever represented in the Church. The religious state makes clear how far the kingdom of God and its deepest demands are superior to all earthly consideration. It clearly shows all men both the greatness of the strength of Christ the King and the infinite power of the Holy Spirit marvelously working in the Church.

Religious Life Pertains to the Life of the Church

Thus, the state which is constituted by the profession of the evangelical counsels, though it does not belong to the hierarchical structure of the Church, nevertheless, undeniably belongs to its life and holiness.

The Hierarchy Regulates the Religious State

45.   Since the ecclesiastical hierarchy has the duty of feeding the people of God and leading them to ever richer pastures, the Church must regulate by wise laws, the evangelical counsels by which the perfection of charity towards God and our neighbor is so singularly encouraged. Furthermore, the hierarchy, following with docility the prompting of the Holy Spirit, accepts the rules presented by outstanding men and women and authentically approves these rules after adjustment. It also aids by its vigilant and safeguarding authority those institutes variously established for the building up of Christ's body in order that they may grow and flourish according to the spirit of the founders.

Variety of Jurisdiction over Religious Institutes

Any institute of perfection and its individual members may be removed from the jurisdiction of the local ordinaries by the Supreme Pontiff and subjected to himself alone. This is done in virtue of his primacy over the entire Church in order to provide more fully for the necessities of the entire flock of the Lord and in consideration of the common good. In like manner, these institutes may be left or committed to the charge of the relevant patriarchical authority. The members of these institutes, in fulfilling their obligation to the Church in accordance with their particular form of life, ought to show reverence and obedience to bishops according to the sacred canons. The bishops are owed this respect because of their pastoral authority in their own churches and because of the need of unity and harmony in the apostolate.

Public Acceptance of Religious Vows by the Church

The Church not only raises the religious profession to the dignity of a canonical state by her approval, but even demonstrates that this profession is a state consecrated to God by the liturgical setting of that profession. The Church itself, by the authority given it by God, accepts the vows of the newly professed. It begs aid and grace from God for them by its public prayer. It commends them to God, imparts a spiritual blessing on them and accompanies their self-offering by the Eucharistic sacrifice.

Religious Exemplify Christ to the World

46.   Religious should insure that the Church can, by their means, daily present Christ better and better to believers and non-believers. The Church thus portrays Christ in contemplation on the mountain, proclaiming the kingdom of God to the multitudes, healing the sick and maimed, converting sinners to a better life, blessing children and doing good to all men, always obedient to the will of the Father who sent him.

Religious Life Helps Develop Human Personality

All should take note that the profession of the evangelical counsels, though entailing the renunciation of certain values which are undoubtedly to be esteemed, does not detract from a genuine development of the human person, but rather by its very nature is most beneficial to its development. Indeed the counsels, voluntarily undertaken according to each one's personal vocation, contribute a great deal to purification of heart and spiritual liberty. They continually stir up the fervor of charity, but especially they can mold the Christian person more fully to that type of chaste and detached life, which Christ the Lord chose for himself and which his Mother also embraced, as is clearly proven by the example of so many holy founders. Let no one think that religious have become strangers to their fellowmen or useless citizens of this earthly city by their consecration. For even though it sometimes happens that religious do not directly mingle with their contemporaries, yet in a more profound sense they are united with them in the heart of Christ and spiritually cooperate with them, so that the building up of the earthly city may have its foundation in the Lord and tend toward him, lest perhaps those who build this city shall have labored in vain.

Praise for Religious

Therefore, this Sacred Synod encourages and praises the men and women, Brothers and Sisters, who in monasteries, or in schools and hospitals, or in the missions, adorn the bride of Christ by their unswerving and humble faithfulness in their chosen consecration and render generous services of all kinds to their fellow men.

Religious Must Grow in Holiness

47.   Let each of the faithful who is called to the profession of the evangelical counsels carefully see to it that he persevere and ever grows in that vocation God has given him, for the increased holiness of the Church, and for the greater glory of the one and undivided Trinity, which in Christ and through Christ is the fount and the origin of all holiness.

The unfamiliar description "the eschatological nature of the Church," is a technical theological expression indicating that the Church will have its eventual fulfillment at the end of time. While it shares the history of the world, the Church moves toward perfection and at the same time perfects the world for the ultimate kingdom of God. In this sense, the Church in the world is in exile and longs for the ultimate glory of God in the restoration of all things in Christ at his second coming.

By his resurrection and the coming of the Holy Spirit, our Lord has established the Church as the universal sacrament of salvation. It is his mystical body and its members are nourished and sanctified by his own body and blood. Through the Church, the restoration of the world has begun. Our sanctity, however, must be worked out in vigilance against the evil one, and we must be ready to enter the marriage feast, lest we be sent to the exterior darkness of hell, against which our Lord warned us.

This chapter is full of quotations from the scriptures that illustrate the pilgrim nature of our life, and expresses the four last things (judgment, purgatory, hell and heaven) in their relation to the destiny of the individual in the context of the whole fulfillment of the Church.

The communion in charity of the faithful on earth, the souls in purgatory and the saints in heaven are all shown here in their unity in the Church. This doctrine is clarified in the description of the witness of the saints to Christ, their union in charity with us, our veneration of them, their loving help to us and their presence joining us in the sacrifice of the Mass.

We correspond with our vocation by mutual charity in fellowship with the saints as sons of God in one family with Christ. The ultimate purpose God has for the world will be fulfilled at the second coming of Christ at the end of the world.

Chapter VII

THE ESCHATOLOGICAL NATURE OF THE PILGRIM CHURCH AND ITS UNION WITH THE CHURCH IN HEAVEN

48.   The Church, to which we are all called in Christ Jesus, and in which we acquire sanctity through the grace of God, will attain its full perfection only in the glory of heaven, when there will come the time of the restoration of all things. At that time the human race as well as the entire world, which is intimately related to man and attains to its end through him, will be perfectly re-established in Christ.

The Restoration of Mankind Has Begun

Christ, having been lifted up from the earth has drawn all to himself. Rising from the dead he sent his life-giving Spirit upon his disciples and through him has established his body which is the Church as the universal sacrament of salvation. Sitting at the right hand of the Father, he is continually active in the world that he may lead men to the Church and through it join them to himself and that he may make them partakers of his glorious life by nourishing them with his own body and blood. Therefore the promised restoration which we are awaiting has already begun in Christ, is carried forward in the mission of the Holy Spirit, and through him continues in the Church in which we learn the meaning of our terrestrial life through our faith, while we perform with hope in the future, the work committed to us in this world by the Father, and thus work out our salvation.

The World Is Being Sanctified

Already the final age of the world has come upon us and the renovation of the world is irrevocably decreed and is already anticipated in some real way; for the Church already on this earth is signed with a sanctity which is real although imperfect. However, until there shall be new heavens and a new earth in which justice dwells, the pilgrim Church in her sacraments and institutions, which pertain to this present time, has the appearance of this world which is passing, and she dwells among creatures who groan and travail in pain until now and await the revelation of the sons of God.

Our Holiness Is To Be Won in Exile

Joined with Christ in the Church and signed with the Holy Spirit "who is the pledge of our inheritance" (Eph 1:14), truly we are called and we are sons of God, but we have not yet appeared with Christ in glory, in which we shall be like to God, since we shall see him as he is. And therefore "while we are in the body, we are exiled from the Lord" (2 Cor 5:6) and having the first-fruits of the Spirit we groan within ourselves and we desire to be with Christ. By that same charity however, we are urged to live more for him, who died for us and rose again. We strive therefore to please God in all things and we put on the armor of God, that we may be able to stand against the wiles of the devil and resist in the evil day. Since, however, we know not the day nor the hour, on our Lord's advice, we must be constantly vigilant so that, having finished the course of our earthly life, we may merit to enter into the marriage feast with him and to be numbered among the blessed, and that we may not be ordered to go into eternal fire like the wicked and slothful servant, into the exterior darkness where "there will be the weeping and the gnashing of teeth" (Matt 22:13; 25:30). For before we reign with Christ in glory, all of us will be made manifest "before the tribunal of Christ, so that each one may receive what he has won through the body, according to his works, whether good or evil" (2 Cor 5:10) and at the end of the world "they who have done good shall come forth unto resurrection of life but they who have done evil unto resurrection of judgment" (John 5:29; See Matt 25:46). Reckoning therefore that "the sufferings of the present time are not worthy to be compared with the glory to come that will be revealed in us" (Rom 8:18; See 2 Tim 2:11–12), strong in faith we look for the "blessed hope and the glorious coming of our great God and Savior, Jesus Christ" (Tit 2:13) "who will refashion the body of our lowliness, conforming it to the body of his glory" (Phil 3:21), and who will come "to be glorified in his saints and to be marveled at in all those who have believed" (2 Thess 1:10).

The Church Is United in Charity

49.   Until the Lord comes in his majesty, and all the angels with him and death being destroyed, all things are subject to him, some of his disciples are exiles on earth, some having died are being purified, others are in glory beholding "clearly God himself triune and one, as he is" (Council of Florence); but all in various ways and degrees are in communion in the same charity of God and of their neighbor, and all sing the same hymn of glory to our God. For all who are in Christ, having his Spirit, form one Church and cleave together in him. Therefore the union of the wayfarers with the brethren who have gone to sleep in the peace of Christ is not in the least weakened or interrupted, but on the contrary, according to the perpetual faith of the Church, is strengthened by communication of spiritual benefits. For by reason of the fact that those in heaven are more closely united with Christ, they establish the whole Church more firmly in holiness, lend nobility to the worship which the Church offers to God here on earth and in many ways contribute to its greater edification. For after they have been received into their heavenly home and are present to the Lord, through him and with him and in him they do not cease to intercede with the Father for us, showing forth the merits which they earned on earth through the one mediator between God and man, serving God in all things and filling up in their flesh those things which are lacking of the sufferings of Christ for his body which is the Church. Thus by their brotherly interest our weakness is greatly strengthened.

The Church Honors the Saints, Prays for the Dead

50.   Fully conscious of this communion of the whole mystical

body of Jesus Christ, the pilgrim Church from the very first ages of the Christian religion has cultivated with great piety the memory of the dead, and "because it is a holy and wholesome thought to pray for the dead that they may be loosed from their sins" (2 Mach 12:46), also offers suffrages for them. The Church has always believed that the apostles and Christ's martyrs who had given the supreme witness of faith and charity by the shedding of their blood, are closely joined with us in Christ and it has always venerated them with special devotion, together with the Blessed Virgin Mary and the holy angels. The Church has piously implored the aid of their intercession. To these were soon added those who had more closely imitated Christ's virginity and poverty, and finally those whose outstanding practice of the Christian virtues and their divine charisms recommended them to the pious devotion and imitation of the faithful.

The Witness of the Saints to Christ

When we look at the lives of those who have faithfully followed Christ, we are inspired with a new reason for seeking the city that is to come and at the same time we are shown a secure path by which among the vicissitudes of this world we will be able to arrive at perfect union with Christ, that is, perfect holiness according to the requirements of our state and condition of life. In the lives of those, however, who, sharing our humanity, are more perfectly transformed into the image of Christ, God vividly manifests his presence and his face to men. He speaks to us in them, and gives us a sign of his kingdom, to which we are strongly drawn, having so great a cloud of witnesses over us and such a witness to the truth of the Gospel.

Why We Invoke the Saints

We not only venerate the memory of those in heaven in order to profit by their example, but still more in order that the union of the whole Church may be strengthened in the Spirit by the practice of fraternal charity. For just as Christian communion among wayfarers brings us closer to Christ, so our companionship with the saints joins us to Christ, from whom as from its fountain and head issues every grace and the very life of the people of God. It is supremely fitting, therefore, that we love those friends and co-heirs of Jesus Christ who are also our brothers and extraordinary benefactors, that we render due thanks to God for them and "humbly invoke them and have recourse to their prayers, their power and their help to obtain benefits from God through his Son, Jesus Christ, who is our redeemer and Savior" (Council of Trent). For every genuine testimony of love shown by us to those in heaven, by its very nature tends toward and terminates in Christ who is the "crown of all saints" (Roman Breviary), and through him, in God who is wonderful in his saints and is magnified in them.

The Liturgy Unites Us to the Saints

Our union with the heavenly Church reaches a noble climax when, especially in the sacred liturgy, in which the power of the Holy Spirit works on us through the sacramental sign, we celebrate together in combined joy the praises of the Divine Majesty. Then all those from every tribe and tongue and people and nation who have been redeemed by the blood of Christ and gathered together into one Church, with one song of praise magnify the one and triune God. In the celebration of the eucharistic sacrifice therefore, we are most closely united to the Church in heaven when in the union of holy fellowship, we honor and venerate the memory first of all of the glorious ever-Virgin Mary, of Blessed Joseph and the blessed apostles and martyrs and of all the saints.

How to Honor the Saints

51.   This Sacred Council receives with great devotion this venerable belief of our ancestors regarding this vital fellowship with our brethren who are in heavenly glory or who having died are still being purified; and it proposes again the decress of the Second Council of Nicea, the Council of Florence and the Council of Trent. And at the same time, in conformity with our pastoral solicitude, we urge all concerned, that if any abuses, excesses or defects have crept in here or there they should to what is in their power to remove or correct them, and to restore all things to a fuller praise of Christ and of God. Let them therefore teach the faithful that the authentic cult of the saints consists not so much in the multiplying of external acts, but rather in the intense activity of our love, whereby, for our own greater good and that of the whole Church, we seek from the saints "example in their way of life, fellowship in their communion, and aid by their intercession" (Local Preface). On the other hand, let them teach the faithful that our fellowship with those in heaven, understood in the fuller light of faith, in no sense weakens, but conversely, makes richer the divine worship we give to God the Father through Christ, in the Spirit.

The Church Fulfilled in the Coming of Christ

All of us, who are sons of God and constitute one family in Christ, as long as we remain in communion with one another in mutual charity and in one praise of the most holy Trinity, are corresponding with the intimate vocation of the Church and partaking in a fore-taste of the liturgy of consummate glory. When Christ appears and the glorious resurrection of the dead takes place, the glory of God will light up the heavenly City and the Lamb will be the lamp thereof. Then the whole Church of the saints in the supreme bless-edness of charity will adore God and "the Lamb who was slain" (Apoc 5:12), proclaiming with one voice: "To him who sits upon the throne, and to the Lamb blessing, and honor, and glory, and dominion forever and ever" (Apoc 5:13–14).

Introductory Note   Chapter VIII

Much discussion has developed since the opening sessions of Vatican II regarding the place of Mary in God's plan and in Catholic devotion. This final chapter of the Constitution clearly indicates the unique role of Mary in both.

It is made clear to all that the sole basis of our veneration of Mary is the fact that she is the mother of the redeemer, the mother of the Son of God. Being a member of our race she is one with all who are to be saved. Mary is also mother of the faithful, and is hailed as the uniquely pre-eminent member of the Church, and as its type and admirable exemplar of its faith and charity.

Our Lady is prefigured in the Old Testament, and is shown in the earliest traditions as the new Eve who contributes to our life even as the first Eve did to our death. Herself conceived without sin by a special work of the Holy Spirit, Mary gave the Redeemer to the world. She cooperated freely with God in the work of salvation. Through her faith and obedience she was united to her Son in his saving work during his life and even to the death of the cross; she was present at the birth of the Church at Pentecost, and was taken to heaven where she is exalted in glory as queen of the universe.

Though Christ alone is the one mediator between God and man, still our Lady is the mother of grace to us through her cooperation with him in the mystery of redemption. For this reason she is our mother and our advocate, leading us to her Son.

Our Lady is also the type and exemplar of the Church itself. Like her the Church is called Virgin and Mother overshadowed by the Holy Spirit in perfect union with Christ. Thus through her faith, charity and perfect union with Christ she shows forth the virtues of the Church, and is a model of all virtues and of perfect holiness for the people of God.

The cult of our Lady, which involves our Marian devotions, is a fulfillment of her prophecy: "All generations shall call me blessed." Our devotion to our Lady is especially fostered in the liturgy but it has also taken on many forms according to the loving ingenuity of the faithful. The Church has always encouraged such devotion and turns to the Blessed Mother to intercede for us that all mankind may be united in the one Church of the people of God.

Chapter VIII

THE BLESSED VIRGIN MARY, MOTHER OF GOD IN THE MYSTERY OF CHRIST AND THE CHURCH

I. Introduction

52.   Wishing in his supreme goodness and wisdom to effect the redemption of the world, "when the fulness of time came, God sent his Son, born of a woman . . . that we might receive the adoption of sons" (Gal 4:4–5). "He for us men, and for our salvation, came down from heaven, and was incarnate by the Holy Spirit from the Virgin Mary" (Nicene Creed). This divine mystery of salvation is revealed to us and continued in the Church, which the Lord established as his body. Joined to Christ the head and in the unity of fellowship with all his saints, the faithful must in the first place reverence the memory "of the glorious ever Virgin Mary, Mother of our God and Lord Jesus Christ" (Canon of the Mass).

Our Lady, Mother of God

53.   The Virgin Mary, who at the message of the angel received the Word of God in her heart and in her body and gave life to the world, is acknowledged and honored as being truly the mother of God and mother of the redeemer. Redeemed by reason of the merits of her Son and united to him by a close and indissoluble tie, she is endowed with the high office and dignity of being the mother of the Son of God, wherefore she is also the beloved daughter of the Father and the temple of the Holy Spirit. Because of this gift of sublime grace she far surpasses all creatures, both in heaven and on earth. At the same time, however, because she belongs to the off-spring of Adam she is one with all those who are to be saved. She is "the mother of the members of Christ . . . having cooperated by charity that the faithful might be born in the Church who are members of that head" (St. Augustine, *De S. Virginitate*). Wherefore she is hailed as the uniquely pre-eminent member of the Church, and as its type and its remarkable exemplar of its faith and charity. The Catholic Church, taught by the Holy Spirit, honors her with the affection of filial piety as its most beloved mother.

Our Lady in the Doctrine of the Church

54.   Wherefore this Holy Synod, in expounding the doctrine on the Church, in which the divine Redeemer works salvation, diligently seeks to expound both the role of the Blessed Virgin in the mystery of the incarnate Word and the mystical body, and the duties of redeemed mankind toward the mother of God, who is mother of Christ and mother of men, particularly of the faithful. It does not, however, intend to give a complete doctrine of Mary, nor does it wish to decide those questions which the work of theologians has not yet fully clarified. Those opinions therefore may be lawfully retained which are propounded in Catholic schools concerning her, who occupies a place in the Church which is the highest after Christ and yet very close to us.

II. The Role of the Blessed Mother in the Economy of Salvation

The Prophetic Figures of Our Lady

55.   The Sacred Scriptures both of the Old and the New Testament, as well as ancient Tradition show the role of the Mother of the Savior in the economy of salvation in an ever clearer light as if

to draw our attention to it. The books of the Old Testament describe the history of salvation, by which the coming of Christ into the world was slowly prepared. These earliest documents, as they are read in the Church and are understood in the light of the later full revelation gradually present the figure of the woman, Mother of the Redeemer, in a clearer light. Seen in this way, she is already prophetically foreshadowed in the promise of victory over the serpent which was given to our first parents after their fall into sin. Likewise she is the Virgin who shall conceive and bear a son, whose name will be called Emmanuel. She stands out among the poor and humble of the Lord, who with confident hope receive salvation from him. The long waiting for the promise is finally over, the ages are brought to completion with her, the exalted daughter of Sion, and a new economy is inaugurated when the Son of God assumed human nature from her, to free man from sin in the mysteries of his flesh.

Mary the New Eve

56.   The Father of mercies willed that the incarnation should be preceded by the acceptance of her who was predestined to be the mother of his Son, so that just as a woman contributed to death, so also a woman should contribute to life. That is true in outstanding fashion of the mother of Jesus, who gave to the world him who is life itself and who renews all things, and who was enriched by God with adequate gifts for this great office. It is no wonder therefore that the usage prevailed among the Fathers whereby they called the mother of God entirely holy and free from all stain of sin, as though fashioned by the Holy Spirit and formed as a new creature. Adorned from the first instant of her conception with the radiance of an entirely unique holiness, the Virgin of Nazareth is greeted, on God's command, by an angel messenger as "full of grace," and to the heavenly messenger she replies: "Behold the handmaid of the Lord, be it done unto me according to thy word" (Luke 1:38). Thus Mary, a daughter of Adam, consenting to the divine Word, became the mother of Jesus, the one and only mediator. Embracing God's salvific will with a full heart and impeded by no sin, she devoted herself totally as a handmaid of the Lord to the person and work of her Son, under him and with him, by the grace of almighty God, serving the mystery of redemption. Rightly therefore the holy Fathers see her as used by God not merely in a passive way, but as freely cooperating in the work of human salvation through faith and obedience. For, as St. Irenaeus says, she "being obedient, became the cause of salvation for herself and for the whole human race"

(*Adv. Haer.*). Hence not a few of the early Fathers gladly assert in their preaching: "The knot of Eve's disobedience was untied by Mary's obedience: what the virgin Eve bound through her unbelief, the Virgin Mary loosened by her faith" (St. Irenaeus *Adv. Haer.*). Comparing Mary with Eve, they call her "the Mother of the living" (St. Epiphanius, *Haer.*), and still more often they say: "death through Eve, life through Mary" (St. Jerome, *Epist.*).

Mary in Christ's Hidden Life

57.   This union of the mother with the Son in the work of salvation is made manifest from the time of Christ's virginal conception up to his death. It is shown first of all when Mary, arising in haste to go to visit Elizabeth, is greeted by her as blessed because of her belief in the promise of salvation and the precursor leaped with joy in the womb of his mother. This union is evident also at the birth of our Lord, who did not diminish his mother's virginal integrity but sanctified it, when the mother of God joyfully showed her firstborn Son to the shepherds and Magi. When she presented him to the Lord in the temple, making the offering of the poor, she heard Simeon foretelling at the same time that her Son would be a sign of contradiction and that a sword would pierce the mother's soul, that out of many hearts thoughts might be revealed. When the Child Jesus was lost and they had sought him sorrowing, his parents found him in the temple, taken up with the things that were his Father's business; and they did not understand the word of their Son. His mother indeed kept these things to be pondered over in her heart.

Mary in Christ's Public Life

58.   In the public life of Jesus, Mary makes significant appearances. This is so even at the very beginning, when at the marriage feast of Cana, moved with pity, she brought about by her intercession the beginning of miracles of Jesus the Messiah. In the course of her Son's preaching she received the words whereby, in extolling a kingdom above the natural bonds of flesh and blood, he declared blessed those who heard and kept the word of God, as she was faithfully doing. Thus the Blessed Virgin advanced in her pilgrimage of faith, and persevered faithfully in her union with her Son unto the cross, where she stood in accordance with the divine plan, grieving exceedingly with her only begotten Son, uniting her heart with his sacrifice, and lovingly consenting to the immolation of this victim which she herself had brought forth. Finally, she was given by the same Christ Jesus dying on the cross as a mother to his

disciple, with these words: "Woman, behold thy son" (See John 19:26–27).

Mary after the Death of Christ

59.   But since it has pleased God not to manifest solemnly the mystery of the salvation of the human race before he poured forth the Spirit promised by Christ, we see the apostles before the day of Pentecost "persevering with one mind in prayer with the women and Mary the Mother of Jesus, and with his brethren" (Acts 1:14), and Mary by her prayers imploring the gift of the Spirit, who had already overshadowed her in the annunciation. Finally, the Immaculate Virgin, preserved free from all guilt of original sin, on the completion of her earthly sojourn, was taken up body and soul into heavenly glory, and exalted by the Lord as Queen of the Universe, that she might be the more fully conformed to her Son, the Lord of lords and the conqueror of sin and death.

III.   On the Blessed Virgin and the Church

The Saving Influence of Mary

60.   There is but one mediator as we know from the words of the Apostle, "for there is one God and one mediator of God and men, the man Christ Jesus, who gave himself a redemption for all" (1 Tim 2:5–6). The maternal duty of Mary toward men in no way obscures or diminishes this unique mediation of Christ, but rather shows his power. For all the salvific influence of the Blessed Virgin on men originates, not from some inner necessity, but from divine pleasure. It flows forth from the superabundance of the merits of Christ, rests on his mediation, depends entirely on it, and from it draws all its power. It in no way impedes, but rather fosters the immediate union of the faithful with Christ.

61.   Predestined from eternity to be the Mother of God by that decree of divine providence which determined the incarnation of the Word, the Blessed Virgin was on the earth the virgin mother of the redeemer, and above all others and in a singular way the generous associate and humble handmaid of the Lord. She conceived, brought forth, and nourished Christ, she presented him to the Father in the temple, and was united with him by compassion as he died on the cross. In this singular way she cooperated by her obedience, faith, hope and burning charity in the work of the Savior in giving back supernatural life to souls. Wherefore she is our mother in the order of grace.

Mary Intercedes for the Church

62.   This maternity of Mary in the order of grace began with the
consent which she gave in faith at the annunciation and which she
sustained without wavering beneath the cross, and lasts until the
eternal fulfilment of all the elect. Taken up to heaven she did not
lay aside this salvific duty, but by her constant intercession continued to bring us the gifts of eternal salvation. By her maternal
charity, she cares for the brethren of her Son, who still journey on
earth surrounded by dangers and difficulties, until they are led into
the happiness of their true home. Therefore the Blessed Virgin is
invoked by the Church under the titles of advocate, auxiliatrix,
adjutrix, and mediatrix. This, however, is understood in such a way
that it neither takes away from nor adds anything to the dignity and
efficaciousness of Christ the one mediator.

Christ's Mediation Can Be Shared

No creature could ever be counted as equal with the incarnate
Word and Redeemer. Just as the priesthood of Christ is shared in
various ways by the ministers and the faithful, and as the unique
goodness of God is spread in various ways among his creatures, so
the one mediation of the redeemer does not exclude but rather
stimulates among creatures a varied and shared cooperation from
this one source.

Mary Leads Us to Christ

The Church does not hesitate to profess this subordinate office of
Mary, for it knows it from unfailing experience and it commends it
to the hearts of the faithful, so that encouraged by this maternal help
they may the more intimately adhere to the mediator and redeemer.

Mary and the Church

63.   By reason of the gift and function of divine maternity, by
which she is united with her Son, the redeemer, and with his singular graces and functions, the Blessed Virgin is also intimately united
with the Church. As St. Ambrose taught, the Mother of God is a
type of the Church in the order of faith, charity and perfect union
with Christ. For in the mystery of the Church, which is itself rightly
called mother and virgin, the Blessed Virgin stands out in eminent
and singular fashion as exemplar both of virgin and mother. By her
belief and obedience, not knowing man but overshadowed by the
Holy Spirit, as the new Eve she brought forth on earth the very Son

of the Father, showing an undefiled faith not in the word of the ancient serpent, but in that of God's messenger. The Son whom she brought forth is he whom God placed as the first-born among many brethren, namely the faithful in whose generation and education she cooperates with maternal love.

The Church Resembles the Mother of Christ

64.   The Church indeed, contemplating Mary's hidden sanctity, imitating her charity and faithfully fulfilling the Father's will, by receiving the word of God in faith becomes herself a mother. By her preaching she brings forth to a new and immortal life the sons who are born to her in baptism, conceived of the Holy Spirit and born of God. She herself is a virgin, who keeps whole and entire the pledge she has given to her spouse. Imitating the mother of her Lord, and by the power of the Holy Spirit, whe keeps with virginal purity an entire faith, a firm hope and a sincere charity.

Mary, Model of the Church

65.   But while in the most holy Virgin the Church has already reached that perfection whereby she is without spot or wrinkle, the followers of Christ still strive to increase in holiness by conquering sin. And so they turn their eyes to Mary who shines forth to the whole community of the elect as the model of virtues. Piously meditating on her and contemplating her in the light of the Word made man, the Church with reverence enters more intimately into the great mystery of the incarnation and becomes more and more like her spouse. For Mary, having entered intimately into salvation history, in some way unites and echoes the great teachings of faith, and while her glories are preached and she is venerated, she calls the believers to her Son and his sacrifice and to the love of the Father. Seeking the glory of Christ, the Church becomes more like her exalted type, and continually progresses in faith, hope and charity, seeking and doing the will of God in all things. Hence the Church, in her apostolic work also, justly looks to her who brought forth Christ, who was conceived of the Holy Spirit, who was born of the Virgin that through the Church he may be born and may increase in the hearts of the faithful also. The Virgin in her own life gave an example of that maternal love, which should animate all who cooperate in the apostolic mission of the Church for the regeneration of men.

IV. The Cult of the Blessed Virgin in the Church

"All Generations Shall Call Me Blessed"

66.   Placed by the grace of God, as God's Mother, next to her Son, and exalted above all angels and men, Mary took part in the mysteries of Christ and is justly honored by a special cult in the Church. It is evident that from earliest times the Blessed Virgin is honored under the title of Mother of God, under whose protection the faithful took refuge in all their dangers and necessities. Hence after the Synod of Ephesus the cult of the people of God toward Mary wonderfully increased in veneration and love, in invocation and imitation, according to her own prophetic words: "All generations shall call me blessed, because he that is mighty has done great things for me" (Luke 1:48). This cult, as it always existed, is quite unique but it differs essentially from the cult of adoration which is offered to the Incarnate Word, as well to the Father and the Holy Spirit, and it strongly supports it. The Church has approved various forms of piety toward the Mother of God within the limits of sound and orthodox doctrine, according to the conditions of time and place, and the nature and ingenuity of the faithful. The effect has been that while the Mother is honored, the Son, through whom all things have their being and in whom it has pleased the Father that all fullness should dwell, is rightly known, loved and glorified and that all his commands are observed.

The Cult of Mary To Be Fostered

67.   This Holy Synod deliberately teaches this Catholic doctrine and at the same time admonishes all the sons of the Church that the cult, expecially the liturgical cult, of the Blessed Virgin, is to be generously fostered, and the practices and exercises of piety, recommended by the magisterium of the Church toward her in the course of centuries be highly valued, and those decrees, which have been given in the early days regarding the cult of images of Christ, the Blessed Virgin and the saints, be religiously observed. It exhorts theologians and preachers of the divine word zealously to abstain from all gross exaggerations and from narrow-mindedness in considering the unique dignity of the Mother of God. They must study Sacred Scripture, the Holy Fathers, the doctors and liturgy of the Church, and under the guidance of the Church's magisterium, they must accurately present the functions and privileges of the Blessed Virgin which are always related to Christ, the source of all truth, sanctity and piety. They should assiduously avoid every word or

deed, which could lead separated brethren or any other into error regarding the true doctrine of the Church. The faithful should remember moreover that true devotion consists neither in sterile or transitory emotion, nor in vain credulity, but proceeds from true faith, by which we are led to know the excellence of the Mother of God, and are moved to a filial love toward our mother and to the imitation of her virtues.

V. Mary the Sign of Created Hope and Solace To the Wandering People of God

68.   Just as the mother of Jesus, glorified in body and soul in heaven, is the image and beginning of the Church as it is to be perfected in the world to come, so likewise she shines forth on earth as a sign of sure hope and solace to the people of God during its sojourn on earth, until the day of the Lord shall come.

Our Lady and Unity

69.   It gives great joy and comfort to this holy and general Synod that even among the separated brethren there are some who give due honor to the mother of our Lord and Savior, especially among the Orientals, who with fervor and devotion give honor to the Mother of God, ever virgin. The entire body of the faithful pours forth urgent supplications to the mother of God and mother of men that she, who aided the beginnings of the Church by her prayers, now that she is exalted above all the angels and saints, may intercede before her Son in the fellowship of all the saints, until all families of people, whether they are honored with the title of Christian or whether they still do not know the Savior, may be happily gathered together in peace and harmony into one people of God, for the glory of the most holy and undivided Trinity.

Each and all these items which are set forth in this dogmatic Constitution have met with the approval of the Council Fathers. And We by the apostolic power given Us by Christ together with the Venerable Fathers in the Holy Spirit, approve, decree and establish it and command that what has thus been decided in the Council be promulgated for the glory of God.

Given in Rome at St. Peter's on November 21, 1964.
Paul Pp. VI

DISCUSSION QUESTIONS

Numbers following questions refer to paragraphs.

Chapter I

1. In what way is "the Church in Christ"? 1
2. After 20 centuries the Church now sets out to explain its nature and mission. Discuss the reasons for this. 1
3. Describe the Church's place in the plan of salvation. 2
4. What did Christ accomplish in inaugurating the kingdom of heaven on earth? 3
5. How is the growth of the Church, that is, the kingdom of Christ, symbolized? 3
6. How is the unity of the mystical body achieved and expressed? 3
7. What role does the Holy Spirit play in the Church? 4
8. Describe the continuing energy and direction which the Holy Spirit brings to the Church. 4
9. Christ brought the kingdom of God to earth. How is this demonstrated? 5
10. By what means is a person received into the kingdom? 5
11. Describe the mission which the Church received from Christ through his death and resurrection. 5
12. Discuss the imagery which the scriptures use in describing the Church. 6
13. Who are members of Christ's body? By what means are they united to him? 7
14. How is baptism like Christ's death and resurrection? 7
15. Describe the composition and function of Christ's mystical Body. 7
16. What is the relationship between the Church as a visible structure and the Church as Christ's mystical body? 8
17. Discuss the analogy between Christ's incarnate nature and the social structure of the Church. 8
18. How is this institutional Church to be extended and directed? What manner of life must it expect to lead? 8

Chapter II

Chapter III

45. What is the relationship of the pope to the college of bishop? 22
46. What is the relationship of a bishop to his own church? To the universal Church? 23
47. Describe the cooperation that is needed among bishops and among local churches. 23
48. Discuss the the source and nature of the bishops' mission. 24
49. Discuss the conditions under which "religious submission of mind and will" is expected from the faithful. 25
50. What is the source of the Church's infallibility? Who can exercise it? Under what conditions? 25
51. In what form is revelation transmitted? Can new insights be added to it? 25
52. Describe the function of the bishop in ordering and directing the liturgy of the Church. 26
53. What is the extent of the individual bishop's authority? To what is it subordinated? 27
54. What is the relationship of bishop and people? 27
55. Describe the ministry which priests share with bishops. 28
56. What is the relationship between priest and bishop? 28
57. What are the duties of a deacon? 29

Chapter IV

58. In what ways do priests, religious and laity share a common mission? 31
59. What are the specific functions of the laity? 31
60. How does the diversity of function in the Church add to its unity? 32
61. Discuss the nature and operation of the lay apostolate. 33
62. In what way do the laity share in the priestly ministry? 34
63. Explain how the layman functions as a witness and prophet in the world. 35
64. How can laymen use their competence in secular affairs to advance the kingdom of God? 36
65. Discuss the rights and duties of the layman in regard to the Church officials. 37

Chapter V

66. What is the source of the Church's holiness? 39
67. How is this holiness manifested? 39

5/5/–6
119